International Federation of Library Associations and Institutions
Fédération Internationale des Associations de Bibliothécaires et des Bibliothèques
Internationaler Verband der bibliothekarischen Vereine und Institutionen
Международная Федерация Библиотечных Ассоциаций и Учреждений
Federación Internacional de Asociaciones de Bibliotecarios y Bibliotecas

IFLA Publications 91

A Reader in Preservation and Conservation

Compiled and edited by
Ralph W. Manning and Virginie Kremp
under the auspices of the
IFLA Section on Preservation and Conservation

K · G · Saur   München 2000

IFLA Publications
edited by Carol Henry

Recommended catalogue entry:

A reader in preservation and conservation /
comp. and ed. by Ralph W. Manning and Virginie Kremp.
[International Federation of Library Associations and Institutions].
- München : Saur, 2000, VIII, 157 p. 21 cm
  (IFLA publications ; 91)
  ISBN 3-598-21817-6

Die Deutsche Bibliothek - CIP-Einheitsaufnahme

A reader in preservation and conservation /
comp. and ed. by Ralph W. Manning and Virginie Kremp.
[International Federation of Library Associations and Institutions]. - München : Saur, 2000
  (IFLA publications ; 91)
  ISBN 3-598-21817-6

Printed on acid-free paper
The paper used in this publication meets the minimum requirements of American National
Standard for Information Sciences – Permanence of Paper for Printed Library Materials,
ANSI Z39.48.1984.

Printed / Bound by Strauss Offsetdruck, Mörlenbach

ISBN 3-598-21817-6
ISSN 0344-6891 (IFLA Publications)

Contents

VI

Preface

The contributions to this volume from more than 20 countries give a broad overview of preservation and conservation activities, ranging from microenvironments and pest control, through preservation of the oral tradition to the new digital environment.

Sara Gould and Marie-Thérèse Varlamoff present some of the issues surrounding the challenge of digital preservation and highlight current activity being undertaken by some of the major players in the field. Colin Webb reports on the approach the National Library of Australia has taken in developing its programme for the preservation of digital information, the PANDORA (Preserving and Accessing Networked Documentary Resources in Australia) project; and Jan Lyall discusses the establishment of a national programme for preserving documentary heritage.

The texts by George Boston and Dietrich Schüller introduce audio carriers from different points of view, Mr Boston reporting on a UNESCO survey carried out by the International Association of Sound Archives on endangered collections, and Mr Schüller suggesting that digital mass storage systems would be the solution.

Three articles on permanent paper follow: Rolf Dahlφ on the rationale of permanent paper and ISO standards, Inga-Lisa Svensson and Ylwa Alwarsdotter on the paper-maker's view of permanent paper, and Beatrix Kastaly on how the National Széchényi Library and the Paper Research Institute together have developed a permanent paper now produced by almost all paper mills in Hungary.

Also to be preserved is oral heritage and this is covered in the articles by Rujaya Abhakorn, citing a project of the National Archives of Thailand in collecting tapes of important royal ceremonies, parliamentary debates and political campaigns; and by Colin Webb on the work of the Oral History Association in Australia.

Helen Shenton describes specifications for the storage and environmental conditions for the 12 million items which have been moved into the new British Library building; and Toshiko Kenjo covers storage at the National Diet Library in Tokyo. Lin Zuzao reports on traditional and modern preservation methods in China, highlighting the use of Chinese medicinal herbs for pest control in libraries.

John Dean describes some of the strategies employed by the Cornell University Library Department of Preservation and Conservation to preserve materials in Burma, Cambodia, Laos, Vietnam and Thailand; and Rujaya Abhakorn reports on field preservation of traditional manuscripts in Thailand, Laos and Myanmar.

Alain Roger and Christophe Hubert report on how digitization aids the preservation of globes; Luis Pavao describes the photographic archives of the City Hall of in Lisbon and working procedures, including the digitization and computer cataloguing of about 60,000 images; and Marie-Lise Tsagouria explains why the Bibliothèque nationale de France decided to implement an on-site automated binding workshop in its new building.

The last article by Marie-Thérèse Varlamoff and George MacKenzie covers the work undertaken by the International Committee of the Blue Shield, which covers museums and archives, historic sites and libraries in protecting the world's cultural heritage.

Ralph W. Manning,
Chair, IFLA Professional Board

Virginie Kremp
Programme Officer
IFLA PAC Core Programme

Sara Gould and Marie-Thérèse Varlamoff

The Preservation of Digitized Collections: Recent Progress and Persistent Challenges World-wide

"The year is 2045, and my grandchildren are exploring the attic of my house. They find a letter dated 1995 and a CD-ROM. The letter says the disk contains a document that provides the key to obtaining my fortune. My grandchildren are understandably excited, but they have never seen a CD - except in old movies. Even if they can find a suitable disk drive, how will they run the software necessary to interpret what is on the disk? How can they read my obsolete digital document?"

That quotation is from an article in *Scientific American* in 1995. We were then living a total revolution, discovering the Internet and e-mail, and everyone was taking bets on how long it would take for paper to disappear. For centuries man had had but one single media to convey information, which was paper, and all of a sudden, within the space of a few years, a whole set of new technologies invaded the world under the umbrella terminology of "digital information". Such a revolution has major consequences in terms of access to information, and in processing and preserving documents, and raises problems that are far beyond technical skills or management strategies.

At the dawn of the 21st century, an ever-increasing amount of information is created, disseminated and accessed in 'digital form. This article attempts to present some of the issues surrounding the challenge of digital preservation, and in particular highlights current activity being undertaken by some of the major players in the field. It is clear that some good progress has been made in developing guidelines and best practice for the preservation of digital documents, both nationally and possibly internationally too. However, there is still much anxiety and uncertainty over the best way to proceed in some key areas, and these particular issues are explored here too.

The emergence of digital technologies in the library and archival worlds has changed many practices in the profession, and in recent years many major libraries have been collecting or producing digital documents: even in developing countries, librarians dream of turning digital, leapfrogging other tried and tested technologies such as microfilming. It cannot be disputed that digital technology has accomplished a great step towards better and easier access to information; the same piece of information can be accessed by several

1

readers simultaneously, regardless of where they are in the world, and far more speedily than previously. The Internet of course allows millions of people around the world to receive the same information at the same time. Distance, frontiers and time limits have all vanished: it could be said that the only requirements for access to information now are language and technical equipment or connections.

The Threats of Digitization

The opportunity to browse from one subject to another, from one Web site to another, and to automate the tedious aspects of seeking information has revolutionised research. Thanks to digitization, a student can now scan a complete collection of Shakespeare's dramas in a matter of minutes, something which would have taken days before the advent of digitization when such a search would have involved laborious page by page research. Libraries also appreciate the space-saving advantages offered by digital collections: the *Encyclopedia Britannica*, on one or two CD-ROMs, is certainly less cumbersome than the print version, and if correctly handled those CD-ROMs will not need repair or restoration like ordinary paper books which are constantly used and whose pages or bindings tend to tear.

Is digital technology, then, a panacea? The answer of course must be no, or at least only partly so. The limitations of digitization for long-term access to information has already been acknowledged, and it is well known that most of the data generated by NASA 30 years ago when Armstrong first walked on the moon has been lost, unreadable now because so little consideration had been given at the time to its preservation.

The threat of obsolescence to digital information is twofold, since there is a risk of obsolescence to both the hardware and the software. What increases that threat is the speed with which technology is changing. It is almost impossible to retain outdated computers or disk drives compatible with certain outdated diskettes or CD-ROMs, and even if this was achieved, who in 30 or 50 years time, would be able to repair them when they break down? Maintaining the hardware would not be enough if we are no longer capable of using the software, or, worse, if we no longer know what software has been used.

Another danger which threatens digital technology is cost. The preservation of digital material is a continual process, and to the initial cost of digitizing the material must be added additional costs for migrating data every five or ten years, if not more often. Too few professionals are still unaware of the economic burden of digital preservation in the overall management of their library. That is one reason why IFLA and very many other organizations and institutions are trying to raise awareness of the issues surrounding the preservation of digital materials.

Born-digital Works Require Special Measures

There are other, more intellectual and ethical issues too in the use of computers to generate literary works. As a visit to the manuscript department of any of the great national libraries of the world will testify, the hand-written manuscript can reveal much more about the life and state of mind of the writer than any electronic document can ever do. Marcel Proust's "*paperoles*", the small pieces of paper which his servant wrote under dictation because he was too ill to write himself, contain many handwritten corrections in the margins, and are of major importance for all those who study the genesis of Proust's literary creation. Victor Hugo's splendid handwriting and the amazing and powerful drawings he used to draw in the margins of the pale blue paper he favored, are similarly full of historical significance. How can the successive versions of a novel for example, or the progression or changes in an author's thoughts, be studied in the future, when the only permanent record may be a diskette containing the final version. No draft, no hesitation, no drawings or doodles. No doubt either that those who will study literary history or the genesis of a book will be at a loss.

The same is true of e-mail. Although it is sometimes difficult to imagine life before the arrival of e-mail, there is cause also to regret the transitory nature of e-mail. A century ago, famous writers may have recorded their movements, thoughts and emotions in letters to friends or family, and these have often been preserved as part of our cultural heritage, helping to set literary works in the context of the writer's life and thought. In facilitating access to information and in reducing the time for information to pass from one place to another, e-mail has made information transitory and non-essential: in doing so, it contributes to the loss of our cultural memory.

It is widely accepted that traditional printed documents, particularly when they contribute to a nation's cultural heritage, should be preserved to ensure long-term access and availability for future generations. Best practice in the preservation and conservation of traditional materials - not only literary materials, but photographs, manuscripts and artistic works too - is already well-established, with organizations such as the UK's National Preservation Office (NPO)[1] playing a strong role in ensuring high standards in this area.

The need to preserve digital documents is of equal importance, and this essential work is now beginning to be taken seriously. Electronic documents are often considered as two distinct groups: digitized copies of original printed or written documents, and works which have no print original, often called born-digital works. The preservation policies concerning the two groups may be different, especially where the original document which has been digitized is also being preserved. On the other hand, born-digital works may also require special preservation measures as they are unique.

The last few years have seen the exponential growth in the number of electronic documents of all kinds. In the traditional arena of printed material, it is obvious for the institutions in charge of collecting and preserving the nation's memory that not everything can be preserved, and that a selection process is necessary and unavoidable. The enormous amount of digital information which exists, and the ease with which it can be created or changed makes selection criteria even more essential, but in a way even more difficult. What should those selection criteria be? Can we be sure that what is selected for preservation now will be what is required in the future? Would this selection activity influence, if not dictate, the main areas of research for future generations? In the case of continually updated documents, for example online or Web-based publications, should all versions of the same document be preserved, or only the final version? What about links to other Web sites? The exhilaration which grips us when we surf the Net, quickly turns to vertigo when we begin to consider the preservation of that information.

One thing is certain: no matter how important ethical issues and selection criteria may be, managerial issues will probably greatly influence the selection. Migration of information is one of the preservation measures currently advocated to preserve electronic publications, but it raises technical challenges, together with problems of staff resources and financial implications.

The Life Cycle of Digital Material

The concept of the life-cycle of digital material was developed in a recent key project[2], and is rapidly becoming accepted as an efficient and useful way in which to explore the challenges associated with its preservation. One of the *JISC/NPO Studies on the Preservation of Electronic Material*[3], guided by a specially established committee, the Digital Archiving Working Group, this particular study aimed to develop a strategic policy framework for creating and preserving digital material". The life-cycle which emerges is broken down into data creation; collection management and preservation; acquisition, retention and disposal; data management; and data use. The study presents the view that the life-cycle concept is essential because it makes it clear that different stake-holders have different interests at different stages of the cycle. What is crucial is that the issue of preservation must be taken into account at all stages, and not just towards the end of the cycle, since the preservation process needs to be considered from the beginning. Raising awareness among all stakeholders of the importance of preservation is one of the key messages coming from the study, as is the need for cooperation between all of the major players.

The resulting framework which has been developed provides strategic guidance to stakeholders at all stages in the life cycle. In implementing the framework, stakeholders are recommended to assess the issues as they relate to their particular stage in the cycle, but also to consider how the various stages are interrelated, and to be aware of the effects of the decisions of one group on the other stakeholders.

Technology Considerations

This article is not concerned primarily with the technology challenges and problems of digital preservation, but it is useful to mention a couple of key reports and developments which have occurred recently. One of the main areas of debate is what exactly should be preserved. Should the aim be to preserve the content of the digital document, or the physical container? If content, then should an attempt be made to retain the same look and feel as the original, or simply to preserve the data with little regard to the physical container?

The summary report on the *JISC/NPO Studies on the Preservation of Electronic Material* says that "cost management principles would suggest that digital material should preferably held in archives in a standard format, on standard media, and managed by one of a few standard operating systems. [..] However, prescriptive standards in the electronic information world have so far failed to achieve full recognition. The emphasis is now on 'permissive standards'". Opinion of those involved in the technical aspects of digital preservation is that a range of guidelines for specific types of material or specific audiences are preferable to prescriptive guidelines which may be too narrow in their application. On the other hand there are proponents of specific technical solutions. Rothenberg, in a report published recently by the European Commission on Preservation and Access (ECPA)[4], suggests that emulation is often the best technical process to guarantee long-term access to digital resources, and even goes as far as to say that this approach "in the author's view, is the only approach yet suggested to offer a true solution to the problem of digital preservation".

Elsewhere, the CEDARS (CURL Exemplars in Digital Archives)[5] project has a remit to explore issues relating to the preservation of and long-term access to digital resources. As far as technical processes is concerned, the focus of CEDARS is not on the preservation of particular storage media, but rather on long term access to the intellectual content of the resource.

ICSTI (International Council for Scientific and Technical Information) has recently focussed on the issues relating to digital electronic archiving of scientific information. A study[6] commissioned by ICSTI looked at policies, models and best practices in the area of digital electronic archiving. The study was concerned with the long-term storage, preservation and access to information that was "born-digital" or for which the digital version is considered to be the primary version. As might be expected, the study was also primarily concerned with scientific or technical material, which is of most interest to ICSTI members, although it was pointed out that the majority of projects relating to digital archiving are concerned with cultural or historic content. For this reason, humanities-related projects were used in a peripheral context in this study to support the central focus of scientific-based content. Four major organizational models were identified by the study, based on differences in the information flow, the management of the life cycle functions of the archive, responsibility and ownership of the data, and the economic model: data centres; institutional archives; third party repositories, and legal depositories. The report concludes that "There is so much activity among various groups that it is difficult to encapsulate the general state of digital electronic archiving". It also emerges that the issue of major concern seems to be that of intellectual property rights, whether this be the commercial concerns of the producers of electronic material, or the concerns over access and fair use in the digital environment voiced by other stakeholders such as libraries and users.

As far as guidelines on digital preservation are concerned, as recently as 1998, Fresko[7] concluded that there were few widely accepted guidelines, and none which cover all the issues surrounding digital preservation. On the subject of preservation metadata he concluded that "we are reluctant to highlight any approach of those [guidelines] reviewed. The field is young, and no approach has a definitive lead". Although research and the development of guidelines has moved on since then, there is still very little in the way of clear international guidelines in this area.

Who Is Responsible?

Heated debate has been taking place for some time now over who of all the many players in digital archiving should have responsibility for long-term preservation of and access to digital collections. Many believe that the creator of the digital object should be responsible: after all libraries often do not "own" the digital material in the same way as they own printed journals to which they have subscribed, so they do not have the same options for deciding on the long-term "storage" of the material. The job then falls to the publisher - the creator of the digital work - to ensure that electronic journals will still be available in the long term, but publishers have never yet had to undertake the work of preservation, and it is not clear that they would wish to begin to do so. If neither creator (the publisher) nor subscriber (the library), then the job must fall to a third party, such as a digital archive respository. This debate has been at the forefront of recent discussion on the *liblicense*[8]discussion list, and is likely to remain so for some time. There is some agreement that it is unfair of libraries to expect publishers to begin to take on the role of archiving when they have never done so before, but similarly publishers cannot expect libraries to preserve material which they do not own and do not have long term access to. There is good reason to expect licensing agreements between publishers and libraries to change in due course to take account of this dilemma.

"A strategy for digital preservation is part and parcel of any national information policy, and it should be integral to any investment in digital libraries and information superhighways"[9]. This comment, taken from the JISC/NPO summary report on the preservation studies, makes clear the need for national digital preservation strategies, and it is clear that a great deal of work is being done to work towards this aim, at least in the UK. The National Preservation Office continues to coordinate the development of a national policy for the preservation of digital material, and to promote awareness of issues and strategies in digital archiving, but at present "the UK lacks a strategy for the long-term preservation of digital information on a scale sufficiently large to support future scholarship and research".

The NPO has established a Digital Archive Working Group to take forward the work involved in developing such a strategy. The result was the launch of seven different projects to study various aspects of digital archiving. A further one-year project has now begun (from July 1999) in order to follow up the recommendations from that first series of projects. The *Preservation Management of Digital Materials*[10]project aims to define best practice and guidelines for digital preservation, outsourcing and collaborative provision of preservation services. The project will investigate the various remote management strategies that are emerging and provide guidance on these different approaches. The work will also include a cost-benefit analysis of different remote management strategies.

Recording the Digital Collections

Another area of research and great debate is in recording digital collections to facilitate access. Again this is an area where some progress in developing systems, Web-based directories or gateways is emerging, but once again there are no widely-used standards for describing digital collections. The NPO has commissioned David Haynes Associates to develop a *National Register of Collection Strengths, Retention Intentions, and Preservation Status*[11]. The Register would be used to allow decisions to be made on promoting collaborative collection management initiatives, at local, regional and national level. The study uses the model proposed by the UK Office for Library & Information Networking (UKOLN) as the standard for collection level descriptors, and aims to co-ordinate preservation and retention by encouraging consistency in describing collections. This will in turn allow for comparison of collecting policies by subject area.

UKOLN[12] are currently involved in several activities concerning collection descriptions. A review of existing practice is soon to be published which takes a detailed look at the state of the art for collection description as it currently exists in the library and related communities, and a further study outlines a simple conceptual model of collections and the services that provide access to those collections. The report enumerates a set of 23 core attributes for simple collection description, and discusses a possible approach for categorizing different types of collections.

The challenge of recording the existence of digital collections, and making them widely accessible, is one which has no easy answers. Just as the trend for digitizing traditional library collections appears unstoppable, so there is a growing number of projects and programmes which aim to record what digitization activity has taken or is taking place. Some of these aim to identify important collections and to encourage their digitization, while some simply record existing digital collections. Many are national in their coverage, some aim to be international; some have specific subject coverage or are limited by some other content criteria.

What does not appear to exist is very much coordination between these projects. While the stated aim of many inventories is to reduce duplication of effort when digitizing collections, there appears to be no attempt to avoid duplication of effort when creating the inventories themselves, since little regard appears to be paid to what type of directory or inventory exists already. Unless interoperability, or at least cooperation, between different inventories is given high priority, it is difficult to see how duplication of digitization effort can be reduced.

The IFLA – UNESCO Survey

One such project, the IFLA-UNESCO Survey on Digitization and Preservation, being carried out jointly by IFLA PAC (Preservation and Conservation) and IFLA UAP (Universal Availability of Publications) in the framework of UNESCO's "Memory of the World" Programme, aims to register digitized collections of culturally significant heritage material across the world. The project has already undertaken a survey[13] to examine current activity in the area of digitization worldwide, and has more recently developed a Web-based "Directory of Digitised Library Collections"[14]. The Directory aims to list major cultural heritage library collections which have been digitised. As part of the "Memory of the World" Programme, the emphasis is on cultural heritage collections and major libraries and other important cultural institutions.

The challenges which the development of this particular Directory have raised are reflective of very many similar inventory type finding tools. Within IFLA, it was clear that many such projects were being undertaken with broadly similar aims, while cooperation between the various projects was not taking place. The fear that these projects being carried out in isolation were not effective in providing information about what had been digitized led to a meeting of interested groups, which took place during the 1999 IFLA General Conference in Bangkok.

The aims of the meeting were to inform each other about the various inventory projects currently in progress; to identify areas of mutual concern; to consider what benefit there would be in attempting to coordinate the work of the various projects; and to recognize the need for consistency between different inventories and to encourage interoperability.

The meeting recognized that there is a need for some sort of listing of digitized collections: just as bibliographies are essential for recording a nation's output, or the holdings of a particular library, then so is it necessary to record digital collections in some way. However it is clear that creating an inventory such as the IFLA/UNESCO Directory is fraught with challenges, making it essential to establish the scope of the directory at the very beginning. Basic questions, such as the level at which collections are described, are key to the development of an effective database, but it proves very difficult to set the record creation at the correct level.

Where a national inventory already exists, such as the Canadian National Digital Inventory, it would seem pointless to create a large number of collection-level records in an international database, when one link direct to the Canadian national inventory would offer the same range of information. On the other hand, to offer different levels of searchable records in an international database, depending purely on the existence or otherwise of a national inventory, would create an unbalanced service, where subject searches would reveal large numbers or records for those countries whose collections were recorded individually, and no 'hits' at all for countries for which the only entry was a link to the national inventory, hosted elsewhere on the Internet.

The meeting agreed that interoperability between inventories should be a target, but it was recognized in these circumstances that for those project which had already begun, this was too late to be considered in detail. The IFLA/UNESCO Directory, for example, was required to remain within the framework of its contract with UNESCO, and could not at this stage embark on developing the database to conform to any international standards. While this was regrettable, lessons could be learned in this area, and it was generally agreed that no new inventory-type projects should begin without taking into account international guidelines or advice on best practice which existed already, and without relating new inventories to those already in existence.

As the IFLA inventories meeting concluded, perhaps the biggest factor in reaching agreement in areas like digital preservation is cooperation between all of the major players. This has been recognized by, among others, PADI[15] (Preserving Access to Digital Information) in Australia, which has recently established a new discussion list, padiforum-l[16], for the exchange of news and ideas about digital preservation issues. PADI considers that a collaborative approach to guaranteeing long-term access is essential, and is keen to develop collaborative agreements to achieve this aim. In Australia, guidelines have been developed to select online publications of national significance to which long-term access should be ensured. Priority is given to "authoritative publications with long-term research value", and the guidelines cover the preservation of links between sites and the preservation of the constituent parts of larger sites. The Australian statement of principles include cooperation, distributed responsibility and the adoption of best practice and standards.

In conclusion, it is clear that a great deal of intense debate is under way concerning all areas of digital preservation. This is as it should be since clearly cooperation and collaboration are key elements in guaranteeing long-term solutions to the thorny issues surrounding this area. The JISC/NPO synthesis of the digital preservation studies produced a list of recommendations which should ensure that work in this area will be full and energetic in the near future. In particular, the two key areas in which further work must be carried out can be seen as *cooperation* and the *development of standards:*

- Awareness must continue to be raised in order for the issues to continue to be explored and solutions sought.
- Communication must be encouraged. The newly established *padiforum-l* discussion list, and discussions such as the meeting of inventory developers held in Bangkok in August 1999 are good examples of how communication is essential to ensure full understanding and cooperation over key issues.
- The development of standards and guidelines is essential to ensure a continued move towards consistency and the establishment of best practice.

References

1. <www.bl.uk/services/preservation>.
2. Beagrie, N. and D. Greenstein: *A Strategic Policy Framework for Creating and Preserving Digital Collections.* British Library Research and Innovation Report 107. London: The British Library, 1998.
3. Feeney, Mary (ed.). *Digital Culture: Maximising the Nation's Investment: A Synthesis of JISC/NPO Studies on The Preservation of Electronic Materials.* London: National Preservation Office, 1999.
4. Rothenberg, Jeff. *Avoiding Technological Quicksand: Finding a Viable Technical Foundation for Digital Preservation.* Amsterdam: European Commission on Preservation and Access, 1999.
5. <www.curl.ac.uk/projects>.
6. *Digital Electronic Archiving: The State of the Art and the State of the Practice.* A report sponsored by International Council for Scientific and Technical Information (ICSTI) Information Policy Committee and CENDI. April 1999: <www.icsti.org/icsti/99ga/digarch99_ExecP.pdf>.
7. Fresko, Marc and Kenneth Tombs. *Digital Preservation Guidelines: The State of the Art in Libraries, Museums and Archives.* Luxembourg: European Commission DG XIII/E-4, 1998.
8. To subscribe, send an email to listproc@pantheon.yale.edu. Leave the subject line blank, and type in the first line of the message "subscribe liblicense-l *your name*".
9. Feeney, Mary (Ed). *Digital Culture: Maximising The Nation's Investment: A Synthesis of JISC/NPO Studies on the Preservation of Electronic Materials.* London: National Preservation Office, 1999.

10.<www.bl.uk/services/preservation>.

11.Haynes, David. "National Register of Collection Strengths, Retention Intention and Preservation Status". *The NPO Journal* (October 1999).<http://www.ukoln.ac.uk/metadata/cld/summary-1999-11/>.

12.Gould, Sara and Richard Ebdon. *IFLA/UNESCO Survey on Digitisation and Preservation.* Boston Spa: IFLA Offices for UAP and International Lending, in cooperation with IFLA Programme for Preservation and Conservation, 1999. *International Preservation Issues,* 2 (1999).

13.See <www.ifla.org/VI/2/p1/miscel.htm>.

14.<www.nla.gov.au/padi/>.

15.To subscribe, send an email to listproc@nla.gov.au. Leave the subject line blank, and type in the first line of the message "subscribe padiforum-l *your name*".

Sara Gould
UAP
Boston Spa, UK

Marie-Thérèse Varlamoff
IFLA-PAC Director
Paris, France

Colin Webb

Preservation of Electronic Information: What We Should Be Thinking about Now

What I want to do is present the way we have approached the preservation of digital information in Australia, particularly at the National Library of Australia (NLA) where I work. I will also refer to some developments in Europe and North America.It is necessary to make the distinction of how I use the terms "electronic information" and "digital information" because my focus is on the latter, and I will not cover analogue sound and video recordings.

These are legitimately considered to be electronic information, but they are not digital. While there is overlap in the preservation of digital information and electronic information in general, they are best treated as separate fields that can learn from each other. At the National Library of Australia I am responsible for both areas, but I will cover only digital information and how we preserve it.

I also want to distinguish between three types of digital information of interest to libraries: firstly, online publications generally made available over the Internet, secondly, what we might call physical format digital publications issued on tangible media such as CD-ROM and floppy disk; and thirdly, other digital collections such as the files resulting from digital imaging programmes, digital sound files, computer-based record-keeping systems, datasets, and so on. I will mainly cover the first two kinds, online and physical format digital publications, because I think that is where the real preservation problems lie for us.

Preservation - The Next Challenge

Almost 10 years ago I was working for another national institution in Australia, the National Archives, and I was speaking at a workshop on managing electronic records. The highlight of a rather dull workshop turned out to be a dispute between our IT manager and me. As the preservation manager, I said the best we could do was to print out the record onto paper or microfilm, while our IT specialist said, in effect: "Don't be stupid! We will manage this like any other computer-based data." I spent the next five years trying to work out which one of us was right. I eventually decided that we were both wrong, but that I was more wrong than he was. Preservation for digital information will require more than normal IT procedures, but it will have to be built around the technology itself. In most cases, a piece of paper just won't do the job!

In some ways we are still caught up in the same kind of debate. We have made great progress over 10 years, and the steps we are taking now will make preservation possible in the future. What we have done so far has been somewhat like building a whole new library system, so it shouldn't dismay us if there are some frustrations. But the next great challenge will be to ensure the digital information we are archiving now remains accessible in the long term. That is a challenge that still contains many uncertainties.

I take it as a sign of genuine progress that we have moved from a general, rather blurred focus on the difficulties to a much sharper focus on how we might deal with quite specific problems. The simple facts are these: we are still trying to deal with many of the problems we already know about, and we are trying to recognize the critical problems ahead of us. This experience has been reflected in Australia, where many librarians and preservation professionals said even just three or four years ago that digital resources were not worth preserving, and that the task was impossible anyway: where could we even begin? From this we have moved through a range of small beginnings - sometimes deciding to try something even if we couldn't see how to do everything - to a more systematic programme of building infrastructure that could support long term preservation as well as current access.

Infrastructure at the National Library of Australia: The PANDORA Project

In 1995 the National Library of Australia set up a small committee to establish guidelines for selecting online publications we would seek to preserve. In 1996, the Library took the next logical step, embarking on a pilot which was later to become known as the PANDORA project. In PANDORA, (Preserving and Accessing Networked Documentary Resources in Australia), we try to archive the online publications chosen using our selection guidelines. At the start of PANDORA we talked about preservation, and of course preservation is still part of the PANDORA name, but we have come to recognise that PANDORA is archiving these titles. It is a series of early steps in the preservation process, but it is similar to putting a book in a library building - it is not the end of the preservation story, and there is much more to be done. PANDORA has been through a number of phases, growing from a small internal team looking at possibilities, to a "proof of concept" project, and then to a national archiving model that we are now implementing. The project has been widely reported. A much more detailed description, and the PANDORA archive itself, can be found on the NLA Web site.

Pandora's Boxes in the Digital World

Why did the NLA get involved with this kind of material? We believed - and still believe - that Australian digital publications should be seen as another information source to be integrated with existing sources. But they are at great risk of being lost if action is not taken. So we believe that we have to provide the pathways for long-term access. We also believe libraries are well placed to be the main crystallization points for digital archiving. We do not aim to capture all of our nation's digital publications, online or otherwise, unlike some other archiving projects. We believe we can do a better job by being selective, although we respect the views of others who do try to archive a nation's entire online publishing output, such as the National Library of Sweden's Kulturarw project, or the entire global output, such as the Internet Archive.

There are many lessons to be learnt in such an exercise. One lesson we have learned is that things are both easier and harder than they first appear. At every stage we have had to find concepts and models that simplify what looks like an immensely complex landscape. In PANDORA we have recognized many useful models familiar to us from the print world: models which do not explain everything but do provide some help. Collection development policies; classifying and describing information resources; providing access that takes account of copyright; managing risks of loss - these are everyday working concepts from a non-digital context for most of us. In all of these areas, we have been able to say: "What we know from the print world is a good starting point". On a journey of a thousand miles, formulating basic principles has helped us to see where we need to go, and given us the will and the courage to go through the front door and to head out towards the horizon.

But PANDORA is made up of many boxes, each one full of decisions and dilemmas that have been with us every step of the way. The bright side of this is that every difficulty addressed is a lesson learned, helping us to build a workable digital archive based on sound and understandable principles which deal well with the required level of complexity.

In establishing the required concepts and in working with the details, we have relied heavily on modelling - trying to map all the relationships between the processes, the data, database structures, and metadata. For most of 1997 this was our main focus, trying to get it right in a way that would work for a larger archive than the 30 titles that had been taken in already.

In 1998, while continuing to build the archive, (which now holds almost 100 titles), we have focused most of our management attention on two areas that will take PANDORA forward, and will strengthen our ability to handle digital information generally. We want to build a better framework in which we can manage our archive effectively and efficiently; and we want to identify the issues where we need to take action and enlist partners who might be interested in taking action with us. Our technical framework for PANDORA has consisted of a mixture of proprietary software and hardware, open standard tools, and purpose built applications we have developed ourselves. The basic components include: a digital object gatherer called Harvest, which only partly meets our needs; a Web server;
our NLA catalogue using metadata to describe archived objects at title level. Our Web-based OPAC is also the Web interface to the archive; we store the archived objects as a hierarchical set of files on an IBM RISC 6000 computer; and we use some purpose-built programmes that give us limited management of the archive.

It has been obvious for some time that we need to improve some of this to cope with the expected size of the archive. We also recognize that digital libraries and archives cannot afford to have unintegrated systems and pockets of storage when their core business is increasingly to provide linked, rapid, and secure access and retrieval. The need to improve the technical infrastructure of PANDORA itself, and the need to improve the way we manage it and our other collections, have both forced us in the direction of a major systems integration project. We call this our Digital Services Project, and we will use it to collect, store, manage, and deliver all kinds of digital objects the NLA holds, including sound recordings, pictorial images and text files, as well as the archived online publications. We also want to use it to help us manage physical collections of traditional library materials, as well as the physical format digital publications such as CD-ROMs that we are unable to store within the PANDORA project. Our Digital Services Project will not provide storage for everything, but we hope it can give us management systems for most of our library collections, both digital and non-digital. We will be taking our documentation for this project to the marketplace, looking for proposals that address our needs. We are very committed to sharing information on what we are doing, so our documentation will be made available on our Web site once the Request for Tender has been released.

Information Sharing

This provides a good link to our second main preoccupation. We see information sharing as critically important - we cannot afford to waste effort, so we invest some of our limited time and energy in trying to establish mutually beneficial relationships with other people involved in digital archiving. We have established links with many other libraries and projects overseas. To date we have mainly looked to partners in Europe and North America, which may reflect our poorly developed knowledge of what is happening elsewhere.

What are the issues we should be thinking about now? I want to look at this from two perspectives: the issues involved in building national archives of digital publications, and the issues specifically involved in long term preservation.

Issues in Building National Archives of Digital Publications

We have been discussing issues with a number of other national libraries and key projects that we identified as particularly relevant. The issues we have been discussing fall into six areas: collection building, description and control, managing the collection, metadata, organisation and cooperation, and preservation. I want to reflect briefly on each of these, from a preservation perspective.

Collection Building

Under collection building, there are some important issues about how best to get publications into the archive. But there is an even more fundamental question: what is the archive? In an online environment, do we have to move bits and bytes to a particular location, or can we simply leave things where they are and point to them? While we believe there is potential to have de-centralized archives, a model we are in fact exploring in Australia, we are convinced that most digital objects will have to be moved to archiving sites offering greater ongoing security than the publisher's Web site can usually offer. So "collecting" online publications becomes a process of discovering what is being published, registering it in some way, and moving a copy to where it can be preserved. This raises a number of technical, organizational and legal or ethical questions. What technology can we use to capture online publications residing on remote servers? We are using indexing software as a robot to search the Web and make copies in accordance with specific instructions. It is a difficult process with imperfect tools, and we would like to improve the tools we use for it.

Description and Control

Of course, another approach would be to make arrangements with publishers to "push" their publications to the archive, rather than us having to "pull" the publication from their site. This approach is gaining favor in Europe, with agreements between various libraries and major academic publishers, such as in the NEDLIB project, the Networked European Deposit Library, a consortium of nine European national libraries, a national archive, and three large publishers, all coordinated by the Royal Library of the Netherlands. That approach may or may not work with the myriad of smaller publishers populating the Web, although it is conceivable that legal deposit legislation could require publishers of all kinds and sizes to at least register their publications. In Australia we are hoping to have deposit arrangements for digital publications sorted out soon.

At the organizational level, there is a major question about what one should try to collect and preserve. In Australia we have decided to be selective, while some other national libraries, especially in Scandinavia, are trying to archive everything. It requires some hard thinking about what one is trying to achieve, and whether it is achievable.

Of course, copying someone else's publication from their site does raise legal and ethical issues. We have to negotiate the right to do what we have to do; we also have to ensure that the rights of creators, publishers, and so on are not jeopardized by our archiving and access activities. However, the publications become part of the archive, they have to be described and controlled. From a National Library perspective, this raises important issues about the level of control we should apply. Is it good enough to simply make the archive content available to external search engines? We have concluded that we need to include digital publications in our national bibliography, integrated as research resources with the rest of our collections.

Describing digital objects now presents few problems within our cataloguing processes. Cataloguing rules and widely used cataloguing structures such as MARC have evolved, sometimes a little slowly, in response to new requirements. For online publications we have a pressing need for a reliable system of permanent naming in place of the notoriously unreliable URL. Without a more persistent naming system we will continue to lose hypertext access whenever file locations change. In Australia we have been using a PURL Resolver Service to give permanent names to our own archived copies, but we need a solution that has wider acceptance. That might well be the URN (or Universal Resource Names) being developed and promoted by the Finnish National Library.

Managing Digital Collections

For national libraries seeking to maintain an accurate record of a nation's documentary heritage there are issues of version control and authentication. Because techniques such as encryption, time stamping, watermarking and digital signatures are also of vital concern to business interests, it may be that solutions for digital archives will emerge from the commercial sector. We give a high priority to getting the technical framework in place to manage our archive in support our business objectives. When we seek to manage distributed archives there are further complications. We need to think hard about the trade-offs involved. The task of building and maintaining national collections of digital publications may well be more than single institutions can sustain; on the other hand, cooperative models introduce another layer of complexity and costs. This is an important practical issue that we are exploring in Australia. Whatever one's view on the advantages and disadvantages of decentralizing archiving responsibilities, we have to build something we can manage. Good intentions and fine theories are not enough: preservation will depend on something that works, not on something that should have worked but did not.

Metadata

Metadata becomes a vital part of managing digital collections. We have to be able to manage them actively. Somehow we will have to integrate the information we need to preserve these publications with the metadata used to streamline other processes of management and access. There has been much work on metadata for digital publications, most prominently through the Dublin Core series of meetings, which has been developing a set of core metadata elements principally aimed at facilitating resource discovery - connecting users with useful digital resources.

Organization. Cooperation. Preservation

In the preservation community we have different metadata needs, which have been partially addressed by a Research Libraries Group working party on Preservation Issues of Metadata. Earlier this year the working party recommended a set of 16 preservation data elements, which we really need to test over time.

Finally in this broad sweep of national digital archiving issues, there are questions about relationships – whom do we need to bring together? How do we build on the work that is going on in various countries and various sectors? We have decided that someone needs to take a lead, and as the National Library we have taken that role. We also want other players in Australia to take on archiving roles. They will probably include some, although not necessarily all, of the state libraries, some of the university libraries, other collecting institutions, and a few publishers. We don't expect everyone to take the same role, and we don't expect everyone's role to stay the same. There are certain to be changes over time, and some of our partners will only be able to commit themselves to archiving small amounts of information for a few years, not forever. But we still need them to do it, and to do it well. We also need to negotiate agreements with them regarding what happens to their archive when they can maintain it no longer. Despite some early concerns, we are now comfortable with this as a working model, because we think it will reflect reality. Our current national model could be described as a centrally led, but distributed, network of carefully managed but dynamic archiving relationships.

Of course many other models exist for national and transnational action, including the Digital Library Federation of the USA, the Canadian Initiative on Digital Libraries (CIDL), the EVA project in Finland, and the NEDLIB project. There are also some outstanding models for cooperative action within specific sectors, such as the framework for creating and preserving digital archives of the Arts and Humanities Data Service of the higher education sector in the UK.

Libraries particularly need to develop relationships with digital publishers. This relationship can help in promoting intelligent publishing conventions that might make preservation easier, through the use of standard supportable formats, or the transfer of expertise in how the publications are put together. Ultimately, we will also rely on publishers accepting the work we do, because we cannot preserve without copying, which tends to worry publishers.

In digital preservation one can easily get the feeling that development is so rapid one can hardly keep track of it - it was described a few years ago as similar to drinking from a fire hose. And yet at the same time many of the most important issues remain unresolved. This is partly because the material we are trying to deal with keeps changing, so our partially conceived solutions are overtaken before we even get the chance to test them. But it also reflects our failure to learn from each other. The preservation community has had to step out into a wider research community. In Australia, we had come to think that we knew where to look for answers to our preservation difficulties. In this field of digital preservation it is harder to know who has the expertise to help us. It calls for teams of expertise, good communications, a willingness to try things and a willingness to share honest information about the results. It probably also requires a readiness to look in unlikely places for ideas that might work. A good example of this is the work of the Consultative Committee for Space Data Systems, which has developed a reference model for an Open Archival Information System, which has informed our approach to our Digital Services Project and PANDORA.

An especially important relationship could be one with higher education. Whenever we have asked, we have found a deep level of interest among Australian universities, and on a visit to the UK I found a very active research effort under way in many areas relevant to digital preservation. In Australia, if not elsewhere, we have a problem finding the time to establish and maintain relationships with the people doing the kind of research we need. Is especially so in the area I want to separate out, perhaps artificially, as "preservation".

Preservation and Pathways for Access

The steps involved in identifying, capturing, controlling and managing digital publications all play a critical role in making preservation possible, but of themselves they are insufficient to ensure long-term accessibility. There will be a range of threats to digital archives needing to be addressed routinely and at recurring intervals. If we are going to maintain access we will need to develop and commit to realistic pathways that address the threats. Many preservation measures will be included in standard IT practice such as the use of secure backups and the development of counter-disaster plans. However, the certainty of future changes in technology demands other responses that we still need to develop and test. Focusing on the specific preservation issues we are trying to explore, the emphasis here is on physical format publications. We have given them some priority because they are less amenable to the normal IT management processes that will help us with online publications. However, many of the needs apply to archived online resources as well. In an ideal world deposit libraries might preserve everything, but operating in an environment of technical and resource constraints means that priorities must be set. Already there are enough indications of difficulty for us to recognize that it may not be possible to preserve access to everything, and that some options will be costly or ineffective for some materials. Libraries in Australia and elsewhere need more information on costs and options to help them decide what is feasible to preserve and how best to do it.

Research Agenda

We are currently developing a research agenda in Australia to help us answer those questions. For many issues our main task is to find the people with the answers and listen to them. On the other hand, we also expect that even when we know what is possible we will still have to decide what works best in our own operating environment.

Our agenda is framed around three steps:
- Identifying what we already know or believe;
- Identifying the issues needing to be resolved before we can formulate strategies for preservation, and
- Using the research in formulating a national preservation approach.

What Do We "Know" Already?: Options

If we are going to preserve a physical format digital publication, what seem to be our options?

- Documenting the item and storing it with the hope that some "rescue" technology will make it accessible in the future - this does not look very hopeful!
- "Refreshing" the item by transferring it to another copy of the same kind of carrier - this can only be a short term answer.
- "Transferring" the item to a more stable carrier such a CD-R or a more highly maintained system such as a backed-up tape archive - this is also only an interim solution.
- "Freezing" the item by transferring it to a very stable, probably human readable form such as print, microfilm, or something like the HD-Rosetta being developed by the Norsam Technologies people at Los Alamos in USA - this will only work for non-interactive items.
- "Migrating" the item by copying the data and its supporting software to a currently accessible computer format, (with or without trying to maintain the "look and feel" of the original).
- Finding software that will "emulate" the original operating software and make data accessible in a different operating environment.
- Migrating the item to a current operating environment, but maintaining a preservation master copy of the data in its original format so it can be emulated when losses through migration become unacceptable.

How to achieve these, how to choose the most cost-effective and appropriate combination of them, and whether there are other viable options, are the basic tasks before us.

What We Need - Issues to Research before We Can Formulate Strategies

We need agreed arrangements for recording metadata that will help us preserve publications. We need cost-effective ways of predicting and measuring deterioration rates across collections. We have to find cost-effective ways to predict when changes in technology are likely to make collection material inaccessible. We need more information on the feasibility of "rescuing" currently inaccessible materials.

Most particularly we need more information on ways of keeping materials accessible:

- Either by keeping their original access pathways available and operational (what we might call "technology preservation"). In the long-term there is very little merit in a proposition to maintain an archive of hardware and software, but it could be the only strategy available a bridge - pending the development of more sustainable preservation pathways.

- Or, by finding or refering to the user, software which might be a good or bad thing. This is known to be a major research focus within Europe and North America. The main difficulties with emulation are likely to be the costs, which may mean that some less widely used formats are judged too expensive to emulate, and the need to develop emulators for the emulators. It is an approach that could be adopted to shift part of the cost burden to the user, which might be a good or bad thing.

- Or, by migrating publications and their supporting software to each new generation of an operating platform. This is the strategy the NLA intends to focus its own research efforts on in the near future. There is still much work to be done to test reliable, cost-effective migration procedures. We are particularly interested in liaising closely with the CEDARS project in the UK. CEDARS, running out of the Universities of Leeds, Oxford and Cambridge, aims to test emulation, migration and other approaches. The US-based Council on Library and Information Resources is also playing a very important role. They have commissioned comparative studies on digital preservation strategies by Jeff Rothenberg of the Rand Corporation, and by Cornell University Library. We will be watching with keen interest.

Finally, we need more information on issues in managing preservation. In addition to the questions already posed, we need to know:

- How can we identify the essential elements of an item that must remain accessible?

- How do we decide the most appropriate preservation path for a particular item - what indicators can we use to guide our decisions?

- How can we test our ability to preserve?

Conclusion

I believe we have made great progress, but we are still presented with some unresolved issues. We have solved the short-term hardware obsolescence problem by keeping a track of the hardware we need to keep for a time after it has passed out of general use, and by "in-time transfer" of data to currently supported hardware. We have largely solved the media instability problem by transferring data to more stable carriers, which we can do without affecting the data content at all. We have solved the problem of Internet instability by archiving publications in projects such as PANDORA. I believe we have also solved a lot of the organizational commitment problem by strongly asserting the role of libraries, especially deposit libraries which should have a much better chance of maintaining commitment and resources than would other players. And we are even coming to grips with the requirements for handling "upgradable" formats, where we can create homogenous bodies of data that can be migrated in bulk, or efficiently accessed by emulation programmes. I am not saying that all the problems have been solved on those issues and we have some way to go in proving we can manage all of them - but at least the basic concepts are in place. What we are still grappling with is the issue of software dependency, especially where publications use a customized version of software, or software that may be less widespread. For this we need good solid research that will show us what is possible. But I am hopeful. At least we no longer believe we can leave it to someone else, saying it's not our business, or hoping it will just happen.

Colin Webb
Manager, Information Preservation
National Library of Australia
Canberra, Australia

[Mr Webb presented this article as the keynote address to the 9th Symposium on Preservation at the National Diet Library. It was later published in *International Preservation News* 18(March 1999).]

Jan Lyall

National Preservation Programmes: "Such Stuff as Dreams Are Made On"

Background

In early 1997 a questionnaire designed to collect information on the existence and operation of national preservation programmes was distributed to the 150 national libraries registered with the IFLA Section on National Libraries. The responses from countries operating a national programme were analyzed by Mirjiam Foot[1]. Of the 50 responses, 26 indicated that their country did not have a national plan. The geographic breakdown of the 26 responses was as follows: Africa - 6; Asia - 3; Central America and the Caribbean - 3; Europe - 9; Eastern Europe -2; Middle East - 2; South America -1. In a broader and more widely distributed survey carried out in 1995 as part of the "Memory of the World" Programme very similar results were obtained[2]. As has been indicated by Mirjiam Foot, two additional similar surveys have been carried out recently in Europe and the United Kingdom[3]. It seems very likely that with so many similar questionnaires being distributed the poor response could be due to "questionnaire fatigue".

The most commonly cited reasons for the absence of a national programme were lack of funds and expertise (58%) and low priority (35%). The low number of responses from most regions means that it is not possible to draw many conclusions based on regional differences. However, it is interesting to note that 33% of European libraries reported low priority as the reason for not developing a programme but only one of the nine (11%) quoted lack of funds or expertise. This appears to indicate that even for many of the what seem to be more generously funded libraries, national preservation is not allocated a high priority.

Questions were asked about the desirability of the national library playing a central or leading role in the following activities:

- training in preservation and conservation,
- conservation research and material testing,
- consultation/advice on preservation issues, and
- providing conservation and preservation services to other libraries.

The results summarized in Table 1 show that the majority of respondents favour all of these activities being supported by a national library.

Table 1: Role of National Libraries in Providing Preservation Services

Response	Training	Research	Consultation and Advice	Services to other libraries
Nil response	3.8 %	7.7%	3.8%	19.2%
No	11.5%	26.9%	11.5%	15.4%
Yes	84.6%	65.4%	84.6%	65.4%

The Ideal Plan

It is very difficult, if not impossible, to use the findings from this survey to predict what an ideal national programme is considered to be. However, from the additional comments made by the respondents and from published information, a picture emerges of the ideal national preservation programme as one which is managed and coordinated by a central agency, usually the national library, and one in which each library in the country has its own place with identified tasks and agreed responsibilities. It is generally accepted that a national policy will provide the foundation for the development of a national programme. There appears to be an assumption that the national library, or the coordinating body, will have resources and authority to enforce cooperation from all participants.

The Reality

The need for a national approach to library preservation has been discussed for at least 30 years[4], yet few nations claim to have a national programme and many bemoan the fact that they don't have one. Of those nations where one is in operation only moderate success is usually claimed. Why is this? Should all nations strive to develop a national preservation strategy or are there more pragmatic ways to address the issue of ensuring long-term access to documentary heritage? Are there existing models?

Great progress has been made in the past 30 years in implementing a wide range of preservation activities: training programmes have been developed; the profession of preservation administration has been founded; preservation sections have been established in many libraries; awareness has increased; the number of publications on preservation topics has grown enormously: funding has increased; research has been carried out; new procedures have been developed; standards have been adopted; cooperative programmes have been introduced; and national and international task forces have been established. However, this progress is not uniform throughout the world and is not uniform across all types of libraries in any one country.

Many conferences have been held and many resolutions concerning national and international programmes have been passed[5-15]. Shortage of published material on national approaches to library preservation is certainly not the reason for the lack popularity of such programmes. Indeed one of the sad features to emerge from an analysis of this plethora of publications is that over the past 30 years the basic message remains the same: the preservation problem is so vast and so complex that national and international cooperation will be required to solve it. Yet, despite the fact that cooperative programmes are operating, survey after survey shows that few countries have national policies or programmes. It would appear that there is no common understanding on what constitutes a national programme. The reason may be related to the variation which exists between countries. Countries vary enormously in terms of their geographic size, their population size, their racial and ethnic mix, their political structure and stability, their climate, their wealth and their level of development. It is inconceivable that a simple formula for the implementation of a national preservation programme could be identified for all nations.

In reviewing the history of library preservation activities in the English speaking world it appears that the USA was the first to express the desire to establish a national preservation programme. A two day planning conference, attended by about 50 key people, was held at the Library of Congress in December 1976[16] to identify the essential elements of a national programme and to set in place a course of action. It was stated in the closing session that the Library of Congress proposed to move ahead with a national preservation programme. I have examined the proceedings of that meeting and have compared the proposals and speculations made then with the events of the past 20 years.

The first indication that the urgency of the "preservation crisis", identified by the meeting, did not receive immediate attention was that the proceedings of the meeting did not appear until 1980 - over three years after the conference itself. It was however stated in the introduction that in the intervening period two meetings of the Ad Hoc Advisory Committee had been held and that a National Preservation Program Officer had been appointed within the Preservation Office of the Library of Congress. There was also a sobering statement that day to day realities had prevented any grand scheme being introduced and that the National Preservation Program Office was concentrating on making the Library's current preservation programmes, services and contributions better known.

Views Expressed at the 1976 Meeting

The report makes fascinating reading. Much was made of the preservation crisis. Time and time again reference was made to results of surveys and studies indicating that between 30% and 50% of books in American Libraries would self destruct in a few years time unless immediate action was taken. It was claimed that the studies carried out by William Barrow in the 1950s and '60s showed that 40% of books published between 1900 and 1940 would be unusable by 1983. This perceived crisis undoubtedly influenced the recommendations and proposals.

The scene was set for the meeting in a presentation by Gordon Williams, Director of the Center for Research Libraries who had prepared a report in 1965 which pointed out the "staggering dimensions of preservation problems" facing research libraries in the USA. His solution was conceptually simple and logical. It was based on the following assumptions: only a small percentage of library materials received high use; all collections were at great risk due to their inherent instability; all major libraries were running out of space; costs were rising and libraries were reducing their acquisitions; the resources required to microfilm all materials were unlikely to be available; microforms were not popular with users; deacidification would increase the life of all materials and was becoming less expensive; and cold storage could increase the life expectancy of library materials by up to 40 times that which would be expected at normal room temperature. His proposed solution was to establish a few stores across the country which would be maintained at low temperatures and which would house the national collection. All material would be deacidified before being placed in the store and when material was requested a photocopy would be made and dispatched to the user. Deacidification and storage at a low temperature would ensure that deterioration would be slowed down. In the future when improved techniques were developed, treatment of the whole collection could be effected or it could be converted to another format, either microform or a format yet to be discovered.

It is extremely interesting to note that, although certain aspects of this grand scheme were discussed throughout the course of the conference, the total plan was never seriously considered. It is not too difficult to postulate the reasons for this. To have been implemented, it would have required many libraries to have "given up" their collections for the good of the nation, a considerable and perhaps impossible effort would have been required to develop a national bibliographic database, and someone or some organisation would have been required to manage the system. It seems more than likely that the main reason the proposal lacked support was that no library was prepared to relocate all or parts of its collection.

Throughout the course of the conference a number of factors were identified which would need attention in developing a national programme. They are the same as those with which we are all familiar today - the need for research, education, greater awareness, counter-disaster planning, standards, better paper, the cost savings to be derived from cooperative microfilming, the need for a national register of microform masters and the need to only film once, the desirability of involving scholars in the selection process and, although few problems had appeared in the late 1970s, some comments were made about the possibility of microfilm deteriorating sooner than expected. Scant attention was paid to the coordination of the national plan but it seemed to be assumed that the Library of Congress would play an important role. A number of participants stressed the need to tackle the problem slowly, to only attempt achievable tasks while not losing sight of the grand vision. Progress was to be evolutionary not revolutionary.

Subsequent Developments

Twenty years on from that conference, although there is no one national plan in the USA, many of the elements identified in 1976 have been implemented. Although the Library of Congress has not played its anticipated central role many other players have entered the scene: the Commission on Preservation and Access was established and has been instrumental in accelerating progress; the Research Libraries Group (RLG) has become influential; and several States have developed a range of State-wide programmes. This situation was summed up by Patricia Battin when she said "As befits a pluralistic society, there is no monolithic national library in the United States; rather the country's rich cultural intellectual heritage is dispersed amongst hundreds of libraries and archives across the nation[17]".

In examining the lack of success of the 1976 meeting in developing a plan of action it is useful to examine the process and outcomes against a set of criteria for assessing a coordinated program involving a number of partners.

- *Clear definition of task.* No clear plan of action emerged from the meeting, Many ideas were discussed but follow up action was relegated to a committee which appears not to have been very successful.

- *Strong leadership and coordination.* The Library of Congress stated that it would fulfil this role but difficulties were experienced after the event in carrying out this responsibility.

- *Well developed and achievable strategies.* The strategies identified at the meeting were not costed and examined for their efficiency and effectiveness.

- *Commitment from all participants.* No firm commitment was sought from any of the participants at the meeting.
- *Obvious benefits to all participants.* Several benefits were identified in several of the strategies – for example the cost savings in cooperative microfilming programmes.

- *Effective communication networks.* This was not discussed at the meeting but a newsletter was established by the Library of Congress after the meeting.

- *Good management systems.* These were not discussed.

- *Adequate funding.* No additional sources were identified.

- *Satisfactory monitoring and evaluation.* This was not discussed.

To be fair to the organizers of the meeting many of these aspects were intended to be developed after the conference. The fact that they did not suggests that, despite the "state of crisis" identified at the meeting, the establishment of a national preservation programme was allocated a low priority.

Success was achieved in many of the programmes established later by organizations such as the Commission on Preservation and Access and RLG. They focused on certain elements and developed practical strategies for dealing with them. Aspects of the proposed 1976 national programme which were never implemented usually were unsuccessful because it was not possible to demonstrate their benefits in the face of competing priorities. The prediction that 30-50% of the collections were facing imminent extinction did not prove to be true and a downward assessment of this figure has resulted in a less urgent and more rational approach to the brittle book problem. A number of problems including cost and uncertainty about effectiveness has resulted in a less than enthusiastic uptake of mass deacidification processes.

The Australian Situation

Proposals to tackle the preservation of documentary heritage material on a national scale were first discussed widely in 1988. In 1992, with the support and encouragement of the Australian library community, the National Library of Australia established a National Preservation Office (NPO). The need for cooperation at national and international levels was emphasized.

The National Preservation Office was exclusively funded by the National Library of Australia. It had a staff of three and was assisted in its operation by an Advisory Body composed of experts from a variety of fields. It aimed to maintain close contact with all Australian State library preservation groups.

The role of the NPO was defined as "assisting in the development of a national preservation strategy for that portion of the country's documentary heritage held primarily in libraries". The major issues facing Australia were identified as follows:

- *Collection and retention policies.* In recognition of the fact that it is neither desirable nor possible for every library to save everything it collects, it was proposed that agreements defining preservation responsibility for various parts of the distributed national collection would be required.
- *Alternative format preservation.* Determining the relative merits of alternative formats, such as photocopies, microfilms and electronic media, for preservation purposes was seen as an issue which warranted attention at the national level.
- *Bibliographic control.* The Australian Bibliographic Database (ABN) did not provide adequate information on reformatted material.
- *Copyright.* Current Australian Copyright law hindered the transfer of deteriorated material to alternative formats.
- *Legal deposit.* To ensure adequate collection of electronic materials changes were necessary to Australian Legal Deposit legislation.
- *Storage and environment.* Adequate information was not available on the safe storage and environmental requirements for collections in all parts of the country.
- *Disaster control.* Appropriate disaster control procedures were not in place in all libraries holding significant documentary heritage.
- *Standards.* Australian or international standards were not available for many aspects of library preservation.
- *Permanent paper.* Australia was not producing large quantities of permanent paper. That which was produced was not adequately labelled or marketed aggressively.
- *Conservation treatments.* Appropriate information was required on issues such as significance, mass treatments, special media such as photographs and sound recordings; and commercial conservation services.
- *Preservation of digital media.* Strategies to deal with the preservation of digital media were urgently required.
- *Education and training.* Preservation training in Australia lagged behind that of other major developed countries.

- *Research and development.* Opportunities for increasing the range and scope of research activities were to be sought.

These issues were addressed using a variety of strategies and have met with varying degrees of success. Without detailing the success or failure of each issue it can be said that the National Preservation Office achieved success in all areas where it was in control. For example, it operated a successful grant programme to preserve nationally significant documentary heritage in local communities; it produced a regular newsletter; it provided an information and referral service; it convened regular seminars and conferences; it produced proceedings of conferences; it established contact with several heritage and related organisations; and it carried out lobbying and promotion campaigns. Success in other areas was mixed. For example, it is working with the Australian paper producers on issues associated with permanent paper but the conversion of some Australian paper mills to alkaline processing was not influenced by a desire to produce permanent paper; it meets with varying levels of commitment from the different State and Territory preservation groups and has had very limited success in obtaining agreements on distributed preservation responsibilities.

It this regard, is worth mentioning that the Australian nation is a federation of six States and two Territories. Each State and Territory is responsible for the operation of its State or Territory library and public libraries. The federal government is responsible for the funding of libraries in the tertiary education sector. Consequently there is no central control over library activities, but there is a strong tradition of library cooperation in Australia. The relatively poor level of cooperation on preservation points to its being given a low priority in many libraries, particularly most university libraries.

The National Preservation Office also served as the Preservation and Conservation Regional Centre of the International Federation of Library Associations and Institutions. In this capacity, it provided a link between Australia and the rest of the world and assists developing countries in South East Asia and the Pacific.

Current Developments and Future Activities

Early in 1997 the NPO was merged with two existing sections of the National Library of Australia, the Distributed National Collection Office (DNCO) and the International Relations Section. The primary purpose of the merger was to achieve a stronger and more coherent focus in the Library's national and international coordination activities. The new branch is called National Initiatives and Collaboration.

Both the NPO and the DNCO were established in a largely print-based environment, where collection development, bibliographic access, document delivery and preservation were seen as discrete and self contained elements supporting the Australian library system. In this environment the concept of separate Offices, each pursuing separate objectives, was the appropriate structure. In the new digital environment these elements are converging and in bringing these separate Offices together the National Library is adjusting its structures to reflect more closely the realities of the new environment. The global nature of the networked environment has provided the rationale for including the Library's International Relations Section in this new Branch.

None of the activities of the former NPO have been abolished and the new structure is providing opportunities for strengthening the Library's coordination role. For example, the expertise brought to NIAC is greatly assisting in the development of a national strategy for the preservation of all forms of digital information - a task on the top of the priorities list for NIAC.

Suggestions for Developing a National Preservation Programme

Although it is not possible to provide a model programme suitable for all countries, a few basic steps can be identified. However it must be emphasized that there is no right or wrong approach. Often the most successful programmes are developed by the most unconventional route.

The first step is an expressed concern about the loss of a country's documentary heritage. The impetus for this concern can result from a variety of sources: a strong and influential individual can inspire an organisation or a government; it can be prompted by an event such as a major disaster resulting in the loss of documentary heritage; or it can be a general ground swell of interest. Once the concern is voiced, action is possible. Those interested usually meet to develop a plan of action in which responsibilities are identified.

At the stage where the plan is being developed it is worthwhile obtaining information on any existing programmes. It will be possible to determine if any country's programme provides a good model. More than likely, elements from a number of programmes will need to be extracted and incorporated into your plan. There is no simple answer to which element should come first: the policy, the strategy or the detailed programme. In most cases the answer will depend on your assessment of what approach is likely to be the most successful in your country. As a general rule it is sensible to follow the following pattern: quantify the problem; identify the solution; cost the solution; determine priorities; obtain funds; and develop procedures.

In quantifying the problem it is useful to refer to the surveys which have already been conducted. It is possible that, for example, the Memory of the World survey form[18] solicits all the information you require, in which case you do not need to produce your own survey form. Important information to collect includes: identification of nationally significant material; methods of cataloguing and registration; threats to collections; passive and active preservation procedures; known patterns of use and condition of collections; priorities for treatment; details of preservation budgets; and training opportunities. In the likely event that comprehensive information is not available on condition and use, it may be necessary to conduct sample surveys.

The next step is to cost the solution. It is vitally important that the costings are realistic. Many library administrators and government officials are now aware that many of the earlier predictions concerning the disintegration of library materials have not eventuated. It will be necessary to discuss costs in relation to priorities based on an a careful assessment of significance taking into account institutional, regional and national concerns, use and condition. Projects will need to be broken up into manageable components.

Having provided a realistic costing, the next step is to set about obtaining funds. The usual sources are institutional; government and non-government. Non-government sources are sponsorships, private patrons, foundations, a variety of grants and international NGOs such as UNESCO. If funds are obtained administrative practices will need to be set in place and monitoring procedures implemented.

It is possible to develop national programmes without a national policy. A policy will state commitment, define the framework, state responsibilities, describe relationships and provide direction. Experience in several countries indicates that policies are more likely to be successful if they are formulated after some programmes are already in place.

Conclusion

In his summing up of the 1976 Conference at the Library of Congress Warren Haas made the following perceptive comment: "........scholars, librarians and archivists do, in fact, have the responsibility to solve the preservation problem. And that responsibility is not conditional — it does not depend on public perception, or amount of money, or anything else. It is our responsibility and we can either succeed or fail. The rate at which things get done is a function of money; whether or not they are done at all is a function of people."[19]. Over the past 20 years there is ample evidence that not all scholars, librarians and archivists have not accepted this responsibility.

It has often been stated that preservation is too expensive, yet money can be found if a cause is deemed worthy enough. Unfortunately preservation is rarely deemed to be a worthy cause. The lack of popularity for preservation is demonstrated in the following example: an oft quoted reason for the early lack of success in getting paper producers to switch to alkaline processing was the initial high cost involved in conversion from an acid to an alkaline process, yet the world wide public pressure for more materials to be recycled led to almost all major paper manufacturers developing expensive procedures for collecting and using used paper to produce recycled paper.

Regardless of the rhetoric, it is a general rule that it is easier for one organization to undertake a task or project than to be involved in a collaborative scheme. Cooperation is only effective if individual participants receive a greater return on their investment than they would have achieved by spending their individual contributions on their own activities.

The digital environment is introducing many new players to the field of information provision. It seems likely that the OhioLINK system introduced in Ohio is likely to be emulated in other States and other locations. OhioLINK is a consortium of academic institutions which provides access to a range of services including: bibliographic information for all materials held in the libraries of Ohio tertiary institutions, images, GIS data, access to a wide range of electronic sources and a document delivery service to any institution within the state[20]. Will such consortia assume responsibility for the preservation of access to the materials of interest to them? They may become the digital archives of the future. JSTOR which has created a digital record of back files of core journals in 10-15 fields is another example of a new digital repository[21]. Such organizations and consortia threaten the existence of national libraries. National libraries will have to develop new strategies to maintain their role as repositories of a nation's documentary heritage in the digital age. It is wise to remember George Orwell's words: "Who controls the past controls the future. Who controls the present controls the past".

References

1. Foot, M. "Towards a National Preservation Policy", paper presented at the 63rd IFLA General Conference, Copenhagen, 31 August-September 5, 1997. <http://www.nlc-bnc.ca/ifla/IV/ifla63/63foom.htm.>

2. *Memory of the World: A Survey of Current Library Preservation Activities* prepared for UNESCO on behalf of IFLA by Jan Lyall. Paris: UNESCO, 1996. 59p.: (CII-96/WS-7).

3. Foot, op. cit.
4. Poole, F. *A National Preservation Program, Proceedings of the Planning Conference, 1976* Washington, DC: Library of Congress, 1980.
5. Ratcliffe, F.W., Preservation Policies and Conservation in British Libraries: Report of the Cambridge University Library Conservation Project. (Library and information research reports, 25). Boston Spa: British Library, 1984.
6. *Preservation of Library Materials, Conference held at the National Library of Austria, Vienna, April 7-10, 1986,* Vols 1 and 2, Merrily Smith, ed. IFLA Publications 40/41, Munich: K.G. Saur, 1987.
7. *Preserving the Word, The Library Association Conference Proceedings, Harrogate 1986.* R.E. Palmer, ed. London, The Library Association, 1987.
8. A National Strategy for Preservation in Canadian Libraries. Prepared by the Advisory Committee on a Strategy for Preservation in Canadian Libraries. Minister of Supply and Services, Canada, 1992
9. *Advances in Preservation and Access*, B.B. Higginbotham and M.E. Jackson (Eds.), Vol 1, London, Westport: Meckler, 1992.
10. *Preserving the Intellectual Heritage: A Report of the Bellagio Conference, June 7-10, 1993*, Washington DC: Commission on Preservation and Access, 1993.
11. *Towards Federation 2001: Linking Australians and their Heritage: A National Conference on Access to Australia's Recorded Documentary Heritage, 23-26 March 1992, Final Report*, Canberra: National Library of Australia, 1993.
12. *Towards Federation 2001: Linking Australians and their Heritage, Review Meeting, 9-10 December 1993, Report.* Canberra: National Library of Australia, 1994.
13. *Proceedings of the Pan-African Conference on the Preservation and Conservation of Library and Archival Materials, Nairobi, Kenya: 21-25 June 1993.* The Hague: IFLA Headquarters, 1995.
14. *Proceedings of the First International Memory of the World Conference, Oslo 3-5 June 1996.* Stephen Foster, ed. Oslo: Norwegian National Commission for UNESCO,1996.
15. *Choosing to Preserve: Towards a Cooperative Strategy for Long-Term Access to the Intellectual Heritage.* Papers of the international conference organized by the European Commission on Preservation and Access and Die Deutsche Bibliothek, Leipzig/Frankfurt am Main, March 29-30, 1996, Y. de Lusenet, ed. Amsterdam: European Commission on Preservation and Access, 1997.
16. *A National Preservation Program, Proceedings of the Planning Conference.* Washington DC: Library of Congress, 1980.
17. Battin, P. (1992), "As Far into the Future as Possible", in *Choice and Cooperation in the 1990s. Advances in Preservation and Access.* B.B.

Higginbotham and M.E. Jackson eds. Vol 1, London, Westport: Meckler, pp 41-48.
18.   Memory of the World, op.cit.
19. Haas, W. J. *A National Preservation Program, Proceedings of the Planning Conference, 1976* Washington DC: Library of Congress, 1980.\
20. Barber, D. OhioLINK A Consortial Approach to Digital Library Management,
D-Lib magazine, April 1997 ISSN 1082-9873,
<http://www.dlib.org/dlib/april97/04barber.html>.
21. Gennaro, R. de. "JSTOR: Building an Internet Accessible Digital Archive of Retrospective Journals", paper presented at the 63rd IFLA General Conference, Copenhagen, 31 August-5 September 5, 1997.,
<http://www.nlc-bnc.ca/ifla/IV/ifla63/63genr.htm>.

Jan Lyall (retired)
National Initiatives and Collaboration Branch
National Library of Australia
Canberra, Australia

[Ms Lyall's paper was presented during the 63rd IFLA Council and General Conference, Copenhagen, Denmark, 31 August- 5 September 1997.]

George L. Boston

Survey of Endangered Audio Carriers

Introduction

For many years, it was assumed that the polymers (commonly called plastics) used to hold the sounds and images in the various libraries and archives around the world were stable. The film world was the first to become seriously concerned about the decay of carriers - the problem was all too often illuminated by the spontaneous combustion of cellulose nitrate films. This led the Fédération Internationale des Archives du Film (FIAF) to carry out a survey in the early 1990s to locate the remaining nitrate films with the aim of speeding their copying and preservation and helping to ensure that scarce resources were used to the best effect. The survey located about 168 million meters of nitrate film that required copying to preserve it[1].

In 1993, the Library of Congress carried out a sample survey of organizations that store audio, motion picture film and video material[2]. The aim of the survey was to get some idea of the size of the holdings worldwide of the various types of carriers used to preserve sounds and moving images. Eastman-Kodak helped fund the work. Of the 500 questionnaires distributed, there were 159 usable replies. The results showed that these 159 institutions held between them 23,660,379 audio carriers, 3,214,512 cans of film and 2,931,587 video recordings. The total holdings in the world are estimated to be at least 10 times greater.

Background

Much useful information was provided by the FIAF and the Library of Congress surveys, not least that the scale of potential preservation problems was much larger than generally realized. In 1995 at the annual meeting of the Round Table on AV Records[3], UNESCO offered to help fund a survey to carry out a closer investigation of the condition of the world's sound collections as part of the "Memory of the World" Programme.The International Association of Sound Archives (IASA) was contracted by UNESCO and the IASA Technical Committee undertook the actual work. As with the Library of Congress survey, it was by means of a mailed questionnaire. Over 800 forms were distributed - some in French but most in English - and 148 replies were received from 46 countries. The rather low response must be taken as a sign that "questionnaire fatigue" is affecting many institutions. The collections that did respond are to be thanked for their help. In many cases it is clear that much work went into completing the questionnaire.

Exchange of Assistance

As part of the survey, respondents were asked if they were willing to offer help to others and on what basis or if they would like to receive a visit or telephone call to advise on problems. It was encouraging to see that over 30% of the respondents were prepared to offer help; in some cases, potentially without charge. Over 40% of the respondents said that they would like some assistance. Several "pairings" of collections offering and requiring help have been set in motion and others will follow.

Of those wishing to receive help, the vast majority said that they needed advice about storage conditions, digital formats and methods of transferring sounds to new carriers. These are basic matters for any collection and can be the subject of training seminars and workshops. Several of the respondents said that they felt the lack of opportunities to meet and discuss mutual problems with colleagues from other institutions. Although the annual conferences of the NGOs or the Joint Technical Symposia provide excellent opportunities to meet others working in the field, not every institution can afford to send people to these events. I am sure that the position within IFLA is the same as that in IASA. There is a great desire and willingness to assist with the running of training seminars but this is not possible without outside funding.

Results of the Survey

Overall, 19 types of sound carrier appeared in the replies. Respondents were asked to place their collections into three categories: good condition; giving some concern; obviously decaying. The classifications are not scientific. They are broad, imprecisely defined groupings that provide a rough indication of the condition of the collections without requiring enormous amounts of research by the respondents.

Older formats such as cylinders, acetate discs, shellac discs and acetate tapes are where the major problems lie. Of these, the acetate discs and acetate tapes are the biggest potential loss to the heritage of the world. This is because they are mainly unique recordings, whereas the vast majority of cylinders and shellac discs are recordings issued commercially in large quantities. If one collection loses a cylinder, there is a good chance that it will exist in another collection. In general, these particularly endangered categories of sound carrier are best referred to an archive with specialist technical staff and equipment. It is probable that more damage will be caused to these classes of carriers by inexpert attempts to restore and play them than by leaving them on the shelf.

Cylinder Recordings

Cylinder recordings were the first major mass produced home entertainment system. They were made from about 1890 to 1929. Cylinders are unusual in that the stylus does not move from side to side as with LP records but up and down giving rise to a "hill-and-dale" movement of the pick-up. The copying of cylinders cannot be done using the original Phonograph machines. The now fragile cylinders would be destroyed in playback. New machines with lightweight pick-ups must be specially made for the task.

Although duplicates exist of many cylinders, any collection possessing cylinders but lacking technical expertise is still strongly urged to arrange for copying to be undertaken at an institution specializing in the work. A total of 96,855 cylinders were reported from 34 collections of which fewer than 30% were classed as being in good condition.

Acetate Discs

Acetate discs were commonly used by broadcasters and others for recordings before the advent of tape. This means that the vast majority of acetate discs hold unique recordings. The discs were used for a longer period than is generally realized. The BBC, for example, was making some news recordings on acetate discs as late as the end of the 1960s.

The discs consist of a backing plate - usually of aluminium but other materials such as glass, rubber and cardboard are not uncommon - coated with a layer of soft cellulose acetate. The coating is soft enough to be cut easily by a cutting stylus and sufficiently resistant to wear to allow the disc to be played several times before groove wear becomes a major problem.

The major decay problem is that the coating slowly shrinks. If the storage conditions are not correct, the coating shrinks faster. This shrinkage sets up tension between the coating and the backing and leads to the surface cracking. In extreme cases, the coating becomes completely detached from the backing. The onset of cracking is sudden and unpredictable. It depends on the exact formulation of the coating, the storage conditions and the degree of adhesion between coating and backing.
If an acetate disc is in good condition with no sign of crazing or cracking, then it may be played on a modern turntable with a lightweight pick-up arm. A stylus

suitable for use with coarse groove discs is essential. If there is any doubt about the condition of the disc or the suitability of the playback equipment, then don't play the disc. Seek advice. Of the 1,232,118 discs reported, only 10% are considered to be in good condition.

Shellac (Commercial 78s) Discs

There were many companies issuing these discs from about 1890 to 1950. Although the playing and copying of these discs is not as difficult as with some other formats, there can be problems if care is not taken. The danger to this format is also reduced by the number of duplicate copies of many of the recordings that exist around the world.

Despite the common name for these discs, the 78 format was not as standardized as the LP record. For example, the correct player speed of a disc can vary between 60 and 90 revolutions per minute. The size of the groove and, therefore, the correct size of the stylus can also vary considerably. For a period beginning about 1913, some labels, including Pathé and Edison, issued discs with a "hill-and-dale" cut groove instead of the normal lateral cut groove. Of the 1,709,737 discs reported by 55 collections, 55% were classed in good condition.

Vinyl Discs

These were introduced in 1948 and the format is only just becoming obsolete. The category includes long-playing records (LP) (33 rpm) and 45 rpm discs. As with cylinders and shellac discs, multiple copies exist of many of the discs. The players are still available as new and are relatively cheap. A total of 3,539,814 discs were reported by 58 collections and over 95% were classed as being in good condition. Being in good condition does not mean, however, that a disc can be played without care. It is very easy to convert an LP from a good condition disc to a destroyed disc.

Acetate Tapes

Acetate tapes was the first commonly used type of magnetic tape and was in use from the 1940s to the 1960s. As with all recordable formats, most of the recordings are unique. The base material of the tape is of cellulose di-acetate or tri-acetate. As with the coating on acetate discs, the backing shrinks if not stored correctly. It also becomes brittle and snaps easily if stressed.

The fragility of decayed acetate tapes makes it inadvisable to attempt to play them on a normal tape machine. Advice should be sought from an archive with specialist staff before attempting to play them. Instances have been reported of acetate tapes suffering from the "Vinegar Syndrome" - a decay process more commonly associated with safety motion picture films - but none serious enough to lead to the loss of the tape. Nearly 60% of the 784,093 acetate tapes reported by 13 collections were classed as giving concern or obviously decaying.

Polyester Tape

Polyester is the commonest base material for magnetic tape. In addition to its use as a base for a number of magnetic tape formats, polyester is increasingly used for making photographic films. When pure, i.e., without a magnetic coating, polyester is probably the most stable polymer commonly available today. With a coating of film emulsion or magnetic particles the life of the polymer is reduced. The life of a correctly stored polyester-based tape can be in excess of 50 years but it would be better to base any copying programmes on a shorter life expectancy.

In the form of 1/4 inch tape, 70 collections reported 2,161,941 polyester tapes of which 77% were classed as being in good condition. Packaged as R-DAT tapes, 85,202 tapes were reported by 10 collections with almost all of them classed as in good condition. Concerns were expressed by some collections, however, about the continuing availability of the machines needed to play R-DAT tapes.

Two hundred and fourty-five thousand, six hundred and thirty compact audio cassettes were reported by 20 collections with about 75% being classed in good condition. As with LP discs, care is still needed when playing tapes in good condition. It should be remembered that the tape is probably unique.

PVC Tapes

Another common base material for tape is polyvinyl chloride or PVC. This is a stable base for magnetic tape but is not used as widely as polyester. A total of 1,203,235 1/4 inch tapes were reported by 19 collections. Almost all were classed as being in good condition.

Compact Discs

This is one of the most modern formats for storing sounds. The basic format is also used to store images and computer data. A recordable version is now available and is being used by a number of collections as the target medium for access and preservation copies of older carriers. A laser is used to access the data on the discs which means that there is no physical contact with the disc during playback. Again this does not mean that the discs can be handled without care. Despite the early publicity about the ruggedness of the discs, they are still delicate, high precision articles. Copies of the commercially produced pressed discs will exist in many collections. Many of the recordable CDs are unique recordings. Three hundred and eighteen thousand, three hundred and eleven CDs were reported by 20 collections. Two collections with about 25% of the total number of discs expressed some concern about the format.

Other Carriers

Some rare and unusual carriers were reported. Six collections possess a total of 7,800 piano rolls of which only 10% were in good condition. On the other hand, the 5,013 metal music box discs shared by three collections were 100% in good condition.

The report of a small collection of Philips-Miller recordings underlined the need to preserve equipment as well as carriers. The Philips-Miller recorder physically cut the emulsion away from exposed motion picture film to leave a clear section of film of varying width. On playback a narrow beam of light is shone through the cut-away sections of emulsion onto a light sensitive pickup to give an output signal that varies with the width of the clear section of film. The recordings are in good condition but there is no known player in working order in the world. I hope, however, that I will be proved wrong about this.

Acetate Discs and Tapes Are at Risk

The results of this survey have confirmed the thoughts of specialists in the field about the carriers that should be given priority in any programme for copying. At the top of the list are acetate discs and tapes followed by cylinders. Unless particular problems exist in a collection, other carriers can be given a lower priority. A major problem that has been identified is the lack in many collections of the technical expertise needed to identify problems and to take action to preserve the sounds. One reason for the problem is the great number of small collections, particularly in Europe, North America and Australasia. Many of these are highly focused private collections of commercial recordings and they have little or no long-term security. Other small collections, often of unique oral histories, are housed in public libraries. The storage conditions vary greatly and many collections are in climatic conditions unsuitable for long-term preservation.

The provision of playback machines can also be foreseen as a growing problem. The current need to make modern versions of cylinder players will be extended in the future to other formats. The cost of such machines may, however, be beyond the resources of any but the largest institutions.

The survey continues. IASA is still receiving information, albeit infrequently, and would be pleased to receive more. Questionnaires can be obtained from the author of this article[4]

References

1. More information about the nitrate film survey can be obtained from FIAF, 190 Rue Franz-Merjay, B-1180 Brussels, Belgium.
2. More information about the Library of Congress survey can be obtained from the Preservation Office, Library of Congress, Washington D.C. 20540-4500, USA.
3. The Round Table of AV Records is an annual meeting that brings together representatives of FIAF, FIAT (the International Federation of Television Archives) and IASA (the International Association of Sound and AV Archives) and representatives of the AV committees of IFLA and ICA to help foster cooperation in the field of sound and moving image collections.
4. For further information about the survey or for copies of the questionnaire, contact George Boston, Member of IASA Technical Committee at 14 Dulverton Drive, Furzton, Milton Keynes, MK4 1DE, United Kingdom.

George L. Boston
Technical Committee
IASA
Milton Keynes, UK

[Mr Boston's article was originally published in *International Preservation News* 14 (May 1997).]

Dietrich Schüller

Preserving Audio and Video Recordings in the Long-term

Introduction

Audio and video recordings are documents of ever-increasing importance and significance. They are indispensable sources for many scholarly disciplines, the only true representation of orally transmitted cultures and, in a time of ever-increasing electronic communication, they constitute one of the major sources of our contemporary civilization. The safeguarding of all these documents is widely associated with the keeping of books and other written materials. This may be partly because textual libraries have existed for more than 4,000 years, while audiovisual archives have been in existence for only less than 100 years. There is, however, a fundamental difference between audiovisual documents and printed materials which is commonly overlooked. The difference lies in the nature of the documents and in the different degrees of redundancy of information.

Printed matter represents human thoughts by the use of a stock of symbols. A certain amount of redundancy is intrinsic in speech and writing. Letters, sometimes even words, may be omitted without any real detriment to communication. In contrast, the audiovisual document is an analogue representation of a physical status or event: every part of such a document is information. While a speck of mold in a book does not normally hamper the understanding of the text, comparable damage on a photograph would cover up information, and, on a magnetic tape, it could even render the tape unreadable. Seen, therefore, from the perspective of redundancy, audiovisual documents call for a higher degree of protection and security than written materials.

A second reason for increased efforts to safeguard them is the vulnerability of the carriers and their components. A short survey of the most widespread audio and video formats and their specific stability issues will help to understand this problem.

Phonograph Cylinders

Cylinders have been used since around 1889 for original recordings in the academic world and later also as mass-produced recordings for the entertainment industry. While industrial production ceased in the late '20s, they continued to be used for field recording until the '50s! Most cylinders are made of wax; some of the mass replicated cylinders are made from celluloid. There are about 300,000 cylinders in the custody of recorded sound collections worldwide. They are extremely brittle, fragile, and many suffer from mold. Fortunately, most of these holdings have already been transferred onto modern media and thus their contents, which are frequently of unique historical value, are already safeguarded.

Shellac Discs

Coarse groove gramophone discs, commonly called shellacs or 78s, were the main mass-produced audio format of the first half of the 19th century. It is estimated that the worldwide stocks of this format amount to 10 million discs. They were produced from 1898 until the mid-'50s. The discs consist of various mineral substances bound together by organic substances like shellac or similar binding materials. Although breakable when dropped, these gramophone records are fairly stable and there are no reports of a systematic instability problem.

Instantaneous Discs

Prior to the introduction of magnetic tape, which occurred in the late '40s and early '50s, so-called instantaneous discs were the only medium for audio recordings that could be played back immediately. The total number in existence amounts to three million. Practically all of these discs are irreplaceable originals, many of them of great cultural, historical and scholarly importance. Unfortunately, the largest group of these instantaneous discs, the "acetate discs", are at the greatest risk. These discs are laminates of aluminium, sometimes glass cores with a lacquer coating of nitrate or acetate cellulose. With age, the coating becomes brittle by a hydrolytic process: the lacquer then breaks apart, and flakes off. Thus a considerable portion of the holdings worldwide have already been lost. Even if transfer programmes were to be hastily established, further losses of irreplaceable information cannot be prevented.

Microgroove Discs

From the late '40s onwards microgroove discs (vinyl or long-playing records) replaced shellac discs and only relatively recently has this format been superseded and replaced by the compact disc (CD). The total number of microgroove discs in sound archives worldwide is estimated to be more than 30 million. They are made mainly of polyvinyl chloride. No systematic stability problems have arisen so far on a greater scale, but their stability in the long-term, namely for the next few centuries, is unknown.

Magnetic Tapes

Magnetic media in the form of tapes on open reel or housed in cassettes are the most widespread carriers for audio and video data. Early audiotapes used acetate cellulose as the base film material, which is also used for safety film. Acetate cellulose has a tendency to become brittle through hydrolysis caused by the moisture contained in the atmosphere. This brittleness generally constitutes a serious problem in the playback of these old audiotapes. Produced until the mid-'60s, they are at risk, and transfer onto other carriers must be envisaged. Another group of historical audiotapes used polyvinyl chloride as the base film material. As with vinyl discs, these tapes have not exhibited any systematic instability; the long-term prospects are, however, unknown.

Polyester is the base film material which is used for all modern audio and videotapes. It has the greatest resistance of all base materials to mechanical stress and the influence of humidity. No systematic stability problems have occurred so far but, again, its stability over very long periods (centuries) is unknown.

Of the various magnetic materials used to store the information only metal powder, as used in more recent high density audio and video formats, has given cause for serious concern: early tapes of this kind suffered from corrosion but this problem now seems to be under control. There is no precise answer to the question of how long metal particle tapes will remain chemically stable. At this point it must be emphasized that, contrary to laymen's expectations, the magnetic information on chemically stable and properly handled and stored materials is not at risk.

The greatest problem related to magnetic tape is the stability of the pigment binder. A considerable number of audio and video tapes, especially amongst those produced during the '70s and '80s, are suffering from pigment binder hydrolysis. The atmospheric moisture is absorbed by the pigment binder causing the polymer to hydrolyze and lose its binding property. Tapes of this kind deposit a smear of magnetic particles onto the replay heads. This clogs the heads and swiftly makes the tape unreadable. Processes to render such tapes playable again are available, but the restoration process is cumbersome and time-consuming. This problem has been found especially in hot and humid areas where many tapes do not last longer than a few years.

Compact Discs

The compact disc (CD) and its forerunner, the laser vision disc (video disc) have both suffered from delamination, reflective layer corrosion, and crazing. All these problems render such discs unplayable. They have occurred mainly during the introductory phase of these products, and it seems that the problems have now been solved. The long-term stability, however, especially of the varnish on the upper side which protects the reflective layer, is under systematic investigation. More research is also required into to the stability of the recordable CD (CD-R).

In summarizing, it can be stated that the stability of all polymeric materials over long-term periods is limited. This has a major bearing on the stability of audiovisual data carriers: the vast majority of these consist of polymers, in many cases of a sandwich of polymers, where possible interactions between layers have also to be taken into account. It can, therefore, be unequivocally stated that there is no eternal audiovisual data carrier.

The Threat of Hardware Obsolescence

To achieve the aim of "eternal" preservation requires, therefore, that the information sooner or later has to be copied. In the analogue domain, however, each copy differs, if only slightly, from the original. With multiple copying, therefore, the information tends to zero. Even if we assume a 50-year lifetime of an average audio/video carrier, we would need 20 generations of subsequent copying to cover a millennium. Clearly the way to overcome this problem is to transfer all information into the digital domain where it subsequently may be copied to "eternity" without any alteration and loss. Over the last 15 years, since the introduction of digital techniques, great hopes have been expressed in the audiovisual archive world that this technology would offer simple solutions to overcome the pitfalls of the analogue world.

However, the digital revolution has differed from what had been expected. Instead of the replacement of the hitherto few (if not single) professional analogue formats by one or two generally accepted digital formats, the competition between the producers of audiovisual equipment has led to the development of several competing formats which - due to an incredible progress in technology – were often outdated after a comparatively short time and superseded by new developments. This has sometimes occurred even before the market had accepted the previous format. It has been especially true in the development of digital video formats where, to date, some eight formats have been developed, none of which has yet reached a dominant market position.

This situation inevitably leads to the threat of the obsolescence of hardware. There are several audio and video formats of which carriers exist in good condition but they can only be transferred with difficulty and at great expense because of the lack of hardware and spare parts. Advancing technology is a highly aggravating factor in this process. While it is possible, though not inexpensive, to construct a new cylinder replay machine to play these early recordings with better fidelity than any machine of Edison's time, it is impossible in practice to build a CD-player or a digital video recorder once mass production has ceased and the last machine or its spare parts have been used up.

Digital Mass Storage Systems are the Solution

Seen from this perspective, the long-term preservation of audio and video data - if we speak in centuries - is hopeless: the carriers are unstable, the commercial lifetimes of the formats seem to become shorter and shorter and the amount of data to be stored is too big to allow manually operated subsequent copying from one commercially available format to the next, even if only 10% of the amount of data available today is stored. The solution lies in automatically accessible, self-controlling and self re-generating archival systems. The features of such systems are:

The management of audiovisual data as computer files in mass storage systems, e.g., jukeboxes of magnetic tape cartridges; and an open file architecture to accommodate all audiovisual data together with catalogue/content information and written text.

The access time of such systems is not of major importance.

Data integrity is controlled automatically, and copying of the information onto new carriers (refreshing) is done automatically before errors cannot be longer fully corrected.

Once new storage media and systems are available due to technical development, automated migration (transformatting) will be carried out.

First thoughts in this direction had been expressed in 1989/90 and the first pilot installations are already operative within the ARD, the community of German broadcasters, and within archives of the phonographic industry.

While at the beginning of this development there was a certain danger that safeguarding audiovisual materials would be carried out by using the newly developed data reduction (compression) algorithms, it has, at least in the audio domain, become generally accepted that data reduction (compression) is considered to be unethical because of its prejudicial technical effects on the further use of the material.

What Should Be Prioritized?

If audiovisual preservation in the long-term can only be successfully carried out in the digital domain then it would be interesting to have information on the order of magnitudes incurred. A study carried out by the Library of Congress gives an estimate on the worldwide holdings of audiovisual materials which can be used as a basis for calculating the digital storage capacity required for their safeguarding in the digital domain. The result is impressive: the worldwide audio holdings are estimated to amount to 45 million hours, corresponding to 30 Petabytes (i.e., 30,000 Terabytes) of digital storage space; the worldwide video holdings are around 9 million hours, amounting, in digital uncompressed format, to around 1 Exabyte (i.e., 1 million Terabytes). The annual growth rate is reported to be 5-10%. Even in the unlikely event that by radical selection only 10% of the worldwide holdings would be declared worthy of being kept for "eternity" the remaining 100 Petabytes would still be an enormous challenge for the computer industry.

In view of the rapid development of digital systems it does not seem utopian to think that these future storage requirements will be successfully and affordably met. While in the beginning of the debate during the early '90s the biggest available mass storage system was capable of capacities up to 30 Terabytes, current development allows for the storage of 2.5 Petabytes. In principle, there is no limit to the further expansion of the capacity of such systems. Present systems are based on magnetic tape cartridges which are derived from digital video formats, but other media, e.g., optical tapes may be available in the future.

The problem of digitization seems not so much to be linked to hard- and software technology; the real problem is the transfer from the analogue to the digital domain. This is a very labor-intensive process which requires, depending on the difficulty caused by the condition of the original document, a time factor of 1.5 up to 10 of the duration of the document. An average of a factor of 3 must be calculated. Therefore priorities have to be set in the transfer to the digital domain: first, only carriers which are endangered and in frequent demand should be transferred. The question of "what is endangered" is not so easily answerable. While it is obvious that all instantaneous discs and all historical tapes made from acetate cellulose are at risk and must be transferred, the greatest problem today is the prediction of the life expectancy of magnetic tape: while many tapes have survived successfully for several decades, tapes of more recent production particularly have caused replay problems.

Of greatest importance, therefore, is the intensification of systematic research into the life expectancy of audiovisual data carriers, especially of magnetic tape, and also of replicated and recordable CDs. It is imperative to know what kind of holdings are at immediate risk in our collections and which can wait. Without proper research tools we would waste time and money transferring the stable parts of our holdings, while other documents rot away unnoticed.

Research on Life Expectancy Must Continue

As a result of this complex situation, the strategy for the safeguarding of audio and video materials in the long-term has to be twofold: in view of the enormous amount of analogue materials in association with the labor-intensive task of transfer, taking into account the possible further improvement of transfer technology and digital resolutions, all effort should be undertaken to prolong the life of existing carriers to the maximum possible extent. As the complete preservation of all present holdings is not desirable, the necessary selection process will also be easier from a further distance. Emphasis, therefore, must be given to systematic research into the prediction of life expectancy of audiovisual data carriers and into measures to retard their decay. Hopefully, it will also be possible to develop, on a greater scale, measures to rejuvenate already deteriorated carriers.

For the long-term, however, it has become clear that self-controlling and self-regenerating digital mass storage systems are the answer for the safeguarding of audiovisual documents. This kind of concept will also provide a solution to overcome the scepticism vis-à-vis the safeguarding of electronic documents as recently expressed by Jeff Rothenberg. Such mass storage systems are, at the same time, an indispensable prerequisite for the functioning of all kinds of services in the forthcoming information age, to mention only "digital libraries" and "video on demand". Their prices will come within the reach of average budgets. Contrary to sometimes expressed fears, this concept does not call exclusively for huge, centralized stores: it will also allow individually tailored solutions for smaller applications.

Thus, such systems could also be a solution for the preservation of documents in southern countries: while in hot and humid environments conventional audiovisual preservation is generally insufficient due to the notorious lack of funds for the proper air-conditioning of storage areas, mass storage systems, requiring relatively small floor space, could be effectively air-conditioned at low cost.

Selected Bibliography

- Calas, M.-F. et J.-M. Fontaine. *"La conservation des documents sonores"*. Paris: CNRS Editions, 1996.
- Gibson, G.D. Audio, Film and Video Survey. *A Report of an International Survey of 500 Audio, Motion Picture Film, and Video Archives*. Washington DC: Library of Congress, 1994. Partly published in *IASA Journal* 4(1994).
- Häfner, A. "The Introduction of Digital Mass Storage Systems in Radio Broadcasting: A Report on the Progress within the ARD". *IASA Journal* 3(1994).
- Heitmann, J. *"Zukünftige Archivierungssysteme. Fernseh- und Kinotechnik* 507(1996).
- Rothenberg, J. "Ensuring the Longevity of Digital Documents". *Scientific American* 272 (January 1995).
- Schüller, D. *"Auf dem Weg zum "ewigen",* vollautomatischen Schallarchiv". Munich: Tonmeistertagung Karlsruhe Bericht, 1992, 1993.
- Schüller, D. "Introduction to Bit Rate Reduction and its Consequences for Sound Archiving". *IASA Bulletin* 2: 32-35 (1993).
- Schüller, D. "Preservation of Audio and Video Materials in Tropical Countries". *IASA Journal* 7(1996).
- Van Bogart, J. *Magnetic Tape Storage and Handling. A Guide for Libraries and Archives*. Washington DC: Commission on Preservation and Access (1995).

Dietrich Schüller
Phonogrammarchive der Österreichischen Akademie der Wissenschaften
Vienna, Austria

[Mr Schüller's article was orginally published in *International Preservation News 14* (May 1997).]

Rolf Dahlø

The Rationale of Permanent Paper

"Permanent paper" is the term librarians and archivists use to denote the physical substratum for information that shall last for a long time to come. Paper is an astonishing invention made less than two millennia ago in China. It took more than a millennium before the art of the papermaking was practiced in Europe, and some of our European predecessors were worried when this new commodity was used instead of parchment for information. These traditional papers were made from natural fibers easy to separate and form into a felted sheet, and the substances used for making paper gave these papers the necessary properties for a very slow degradation. In those days, the preservation of information had to cope only with external threats.

The supply of the traditional natural fibers suitable for paper did not increase with the demand in the Western world for large quantities of paper in the 18th century. The traditional craft of paper makers developed in the 19th century into industrial paper production with new methods for complete defibring of the new sources of fibers, and the sizing with rosin and alum replaced animal glue or vegetable gums. The traditional papers with their good properties for long-term storage became luxury items compared with less expensive acid-sized papers containing mechanical pulp. These industrial papers were a mixed blessing since they became the impermanent substratum of information that should be preserved for many years to come. Some of our predecessors realized a century ago that the new papers contained internal threats against the preservation of documents. In the age before microfilming, a Norwegian librarian made enquiries for copies of newspapers printed on good writing paper, but I fear that the price was prohibitive even in those days.

The concept of permanent paper is important for many people around the globe caring for the preservation of the records of humanity. When I grew up, an old book for me was normally a book from the 19th century, and I accepted as an inevitable fact that the paper in those books was yellow and less strong compared with white paper of contemporary books. I can still remember the first time I opened a printed book from the 15th century. It had unfortunately been rebound in a recent binding, but the paper was still in pristine condition. My first thought was that the library had given me a modern facsimile to avoid the wear and tear of a valuable object. Careful examination, however, convinced me that this was indeed one of the oldest printed European books. Five centuries had not degraded the paper. It dawned upon me that the history of books had a curious inversion. The oldest printed books had paper appearing as if it had been made a few days ago, and more recent books were not able to keep up their appearances with the rapid changes in color and smell of the paper.

In 1971, I was working in the manuscript department of the University Library of Oslo, then the national library of Norway. I was to organize an exhibition celebrating the centennial of a Norwegian author, and I tried to find some appropriate illustrations in a satiric journal in the beginning of the 20th century. This was an important record of Norwegian culture, but the copy of last resort in the national library was in a sad condition. These pages, six decades old, had an acid smell and broke when my cautious fingers tried to move the newsprint gently. Another task was re-cataloguing the letters to a major Norwegian author. His letters had been sorted four decades before into covers of acid paper made of mechanical pulp. I saw the migration effect of this modern paper on fine writing paper from the preceding century. The first and the last pages were very different compared to the rest of these precious records. The acidity had migrated into the good paper. Conservators used the term acid-free paper in those days, and I asked for acid-free covers for the manuscripts. We used acid-free paper for the copying machines, but not for manuscript covers. After some discussion, acid-free covers were introduced, but these experiences were not easy to forget and became my motivation for participation in the work for preserving the written and printed sources of human culture.

In the '80s, librarians around the globe started many campaigns to increase public awareness of the problems with crumbling books. Some of our European colleagues told stories about jars filled with small paper fragments falling off the shelves in the stacks. In the jars were the remains of the unknown book. No wonder some of the public expected somewhat prematurely the obliteration of the records of culture in a few years' time. In Norway, I chose a slightly more humorous approach to this serious problem. We focused on the image of Bolla the Hedgehog, who is a literary personality created by the Norwegian author, Alf Prøysen, and designed by the Norwegian artist. Hans Normann Dahl. In 1988 she emerged as the principal character in the National Office for Research and Special Libraries' campaign "No to Acid Books!" Bolla the Hedgehog has every reason to fight against acid paper in books, for crumbling paper is an existential problem for her. The story about her and the other animals in a book for children was printed on acid paper: "What will happen to me when the paper of my book is crumbling," she asks. Our message was this: Acid paper will crumble too fast in the passage of time. The strength of the paper will disappear, and it will not stand up to normal handling. Bolla the Hedgehog and all the other wonderful personalities of world literature deserve better fates and not the annihilations in self-destructing paper.

The crumbling of paper is dependent upon the storage quality provided for the paper documents. It is a slow process, but heat and humidity may speed it up. The slow degradation in temperate countries will accelerate in warmer climates. Some people will no doubt regard it as a hilarious fact that I need to spend some of my time with British documents from the Second World War. Discovering the crumbling of records of special operations from 1939, when I cautiously turned over the leaves in 1997 in the Public Record Office, is not very hilarious, however. Not many records have yet reached that critical state after six decades, but slowly many other records from this period will break into small or large fragments, depressing researchers and custodians. We expect paper to preserve its strength for more than six decades, but it is perhaps not surprising that I cannot access the digital information I stored on some of the floppy disks I used a decade ago before I switched to a standard DOS system. Information technology is developing rapidly, and some of the digital preservation problems will accelerate compared to the speed of paper degradation.

It is an illuminating experience to compare some of the pulp types used for modern papers under the microscope. The traditional paper fibers of paper craftsmen and the chemical pulp do not have the rugged and fragmented appearance of mechanical pulp. Understanding that the long and clean fibers give paper its strength is easy. The woods supply most of the materials for modern paper, and only a fraction of the trunk is the cellulose needed for the strong and durable paper fibers. The remaining lignin and other components of the wood can, however, also become a part of mechanical or semichemical pulps for paper. Mechanical pulp contains nearly all the wood, and substituting cheap newsprint by using pulps that are more expensive is not possible for mass distribution of information. Paper can also be recycled, but the resulting quality will depend on quality controls in the recycling process. Papers of mechanical pulp and some recycled papers constitute one end of the paper market, and there are a vast variety of paper qualities from the types that crumble fast to the papers capable of slow degradation with the best retention of strength and brightness.

I have no doubt that we all have had our experiences of fragile papers, and these experiences define two important tasks for us: Retrospectively, how can we preserve the fragile records on crumbling paper? In many countries, especially in the countries with a tropical or subtropical climate, this is a tremendous task. Looking ahead, how can we diminish the escalation of the number of contemporary records needing preservation treatment in a short time perspective? It is this last challenge to reduce future preservation needs for paper documents that is the basis for the international work for permanent paper.

It is a sad fact that organic substances will degrade sooner or later. There is, however, a significant difference when degradation is visible to the human eye after a decade or a few decades, a century, a millennium or longer periods. No paper will continue to exist without any degradation indefinitely if we have the perspective of millions of years in mind. The important difference for people needing paper as a permanent substratum for information will be the difference of papers degrading under normal storage conditions in decades or in centuries or in millennia. Rapid degradation of paper within decades or a couple of centuries is not something that we must accept as the inevitable end product of organic processes. Nature provides cellulose as the building material for the fibers that are the physical substrata for much of the information we want to preserve in libraries and archives. Nature's fibers represent a potential for both problems and their solutions. Used wisely, these fibers may last for a very long time. Unfortunately not all of nature's fibers are used wisely. The chemical composition of many papers too often causes rapid degradation. Degradation is, of course, the main preservation problem of paper documents from the last part of the 19th century and this century. "Degradation" is the cool and calculated term of paper science denoting what we otherwise call the "crumbling of paper."

For long-term storage of information, paper and other traditional media are still the optimum substrata compared to the relatively short-time perspective of digital storage and the fast changes of information technology. Even acid-sized papers normally have a longer expected lifespan than the lifespan of many digital media. Use of such permanent paper will be one way of delaying the degradation of future publications that will affect all organic material in the end. The word "permanent" in relation to paper should not be interpreted as something that will last forever, and the term ought not to be used in the sense of "perennial" or "infinite". "Permanence" is the ability to remain chemically and physically stable over long periods of time. "Permanent paper" will therefore undergo little or no change in strength and optical properties that affect use during long-term storage in libraries, archives and other protected environments.

Defining the technical requirements for permanent paper is difficult. The problem of making a standard for such requirements is the fact that there is no single direct test revealing paper permanence. Some experts have suggested that a standard could be based on accelerated aging tests alone. These tests take time, and the experts are still discussing the difficulties in defining a standardized procedure that will indicate future degradation in normal storage conditions and predict the expected lifespan of a document. Nothing much happens when papers are exposed to a climate of 80°C and a relative humidity of 65%. In some papers containing lignin there is little loss in paper strength after accelerated aging in this climate, but the optical properties may at the same time be negatively affected, indicating that defining these papers as a permanent substratum for information in a long-time perspective is difficult. More of the degradative changes we expect in paper in real time will manifest themselves when paper is exposed to a climate of 90°C and a relative humidity of 50%.

There are many different causes of paper degradation. Acid hydrolysis is only one of many chemical and physical degradation processes that produce crumbling paper. Neutral or alkaline sizing and some calcium carbonate added to paper will restrain the acid hydrolysis. There are, however, many other degradative processes in paper such as oxidative decomposition, cross-linking reactions, changes in the structure of the cellulose, photochemical aging reactions, physical aging and damage by micro-organisms. All these processes contributed to the effects I observed when my hands opened the yellow, withering pages of the six-decade old satiric journal. My hands did not cause the damage, but this damage was the result of the chemical process that started when the paper was made. This 20th century paper had a low initial strength and a chemical composition that started the degradation process already in the paper machine.

Finding a single method that predicts in a short time the expected lifespan of paper for many centuries to come is difficult. We will probably have to wait for many years before this methodical problem is resolved, and we have a method calibrated with the observations of real time degradation in normal storage conditions.

ISO has developed two relevant international standards, ISO 9706 for permanent paper, and ISO 11108 for archival paper. Some critics want a higher Kappa number in ISO 9706 to allow paper based on new high yield semichemical pulps to be included as permanent papers. An alkaline sized paper made of these pulps will degrade slower than an acid sized paper made of groundwood. The Kappa number measures the tendency to become oxidized. Accepting papers that are likely to be oxidized as permanent paper may therefore be difficult. The standard has no requirements safeguarding discoloration of permanent paper. By demanding a Kappa number of less than 5.0 it was not necessary to introduce a technical requirement regarding color changes, which we have to expect in paper containing lignin. If the Kappa number should be increased, new technical requirements limiting future discoloration must be considered.

I find another form of criticism against the requirements of ISO 9706 more disturbing, and it is very difficult to find any commercial interest behind this criticism. When voting on ISO 9706, some national members wanted additional requirements to safeguard paper permanence. The presence of traces of some metals in paper will serve as a catalyst for some of the degradation processes and may affect the storage properties of paper. There may be a need for defining a maximum level of traces of some metals in permanent paper. I understand this concern, and I hope that more evidence regarding such defects of the standard will be available when ISO 9706 comes up for the periodic revision ISO has instituted for all international standards.

When I signed the form authorizing the publication of ISO 9706, I hoped that the international standard for paper permanence would become a starting point to diminish the escalation of the number of contemporary records needing preservation treatment in a short time perspective. I was hoping that many books would be published on permanent paper, reducing the workload for conservators in the future. Some of these effects had already come when we were preparing ISO 9706 in close cooperation with experts from the paper trade. Many paper mills in the Western world changed the production process from acid sizing to alkaline sizing before ISO 9706 was published. In Europe, nearly every fine paper is permanent according to ISO 9706. Only one mill produces coated paper with an acid core. Many mills producing paper containing groundwood or semichemical pulps have switched to alkaline sizing. Thus many Western papers are permanent or have improved storage properties compared with the acid sized paper produced a few decades ago.

Does this change in the European paper trade suggest that all contemporary European books are published on permanent paper? I wish I could give an affirmative answer to this question. Few publishers have adopted a rational policy for using permanent paper for books that will be retained for a long period in libraries. If a book contains illustrations, it is nearly impossible for the publisher to avoid using permanent paper when it is printed in Europe. If a book only contains text, the publisher will often print the book on paper containing groundwood or semichemical pulps. This policy varies from country to country. In Norway publishers used to print fiction on fine paper, but nowadays they prefer to issue fiction on groundwood paper. In Denmark, on the other hand, much of the fiction is published on permanent paper. Are Danish publishers wiser than their Norwegian counterparts? A major Danish printing press has standardized its stock of paper, and a book with groundwood paper will cost more than a book with permanent paper from this printing press. Publishers producing fiction on permanent paper from this printing press cash in on standardization that benefits many of the concerned parties.

This is an important reminder for us that wise decisions are not always made only with the eyes fixed on avoiding conservation expenses in a distant future. Not all publishers have a long time perspective on the cultural importance of their business activities, but many of them have a concern for the red and black figures of their accounts. The paper mills did not switch from acid sizing to alkaline sizing to please the minority caring for the long-term storage properties of paper, but this change improved the process and reduced some of the running costs of the paper machines.

A standard is not a permanent document to remain unchanged forever. Even a standard for permanent paper cannot be viewed as something permanent and not subject to any changes. The concept of permanent paper was coined by many of our colleagues who had experienced the crumbling of important documents. I think it is important that an international standard for paper permanence must be trusted by the preservation community. This is the community that sees the need of long-term storage of paper documents. If the international standard for paper permanence will be changed in such a way that the preservation community no longer promotes the standard, I see no further need for such a standard. If, on the other hand, a revised standard for paper permanence incorporates new knowledge that will make it easier for us to predict the expected lifespan of paper documents in normal storage conditions, I shall be very happy to see a revised standard that commands the trust of the preservation community, and that promotes better products from the paper mills around the world.

In one European country a clever man coined the expression "the office with no paper" to express his hopes for a new, digital way of handling affairs. After a couple of years, this man became the chief executive of one of the biggest companies producing paper in his country. The consumption of paper is increasing with the new information technology. I am probably not the only person needing to print my documents in order to see what I have been writing on my keyboard. Some people try to find permanent solutions preserving all digital information, and some of them want to print it on paper or microfilm as the copy of last resort.

Paper has been a precious commodity for two millennia. In a changing world, there is a case for preserving information on permanent paper. Not all copies of a document need to be on permanent paper. A copy on permanent paper stored in a safe environment may preserve information for a very long time. We do not need permanent paper for every document, but we need permanent paper for all the information that will become the heritage of generations to come. Permanent paper is an important concept for the long-term storage of information, and a revision of the requirements for permanent paper must safeguard the long-term preservation of information for the generations to come. Perhaps these generations can afford to lose the book of Bolla the Hedgehog, but they should certainly not lose too much of the world literature and all the other information that will become the record of humanity.

Rolf Dahlø
Riksbiblioteketsenesten,
Oslo, Norway

[Mr Dahlø's paper was presented during the 64th IFLA General Conference, Amsterdam, Netherlands, 16-21 August 1998.]

Inga-Lisa Svensson and Ylwa Alwarsdotter

A Papermaker's View of the Standard of Permanent Paper, ISO 9706

The History of Papermaking

"Quelle honte pour notre époque, de fabriquer des livres sans durée!" "What a shame for our time that books without durability are manufactured." When young Daniel proposed to the girl of his heart in Honeré de Balzac's *Illusions Perdues Part 1* he said this. The scene outside the papermill where he worked and it happened in 1820. The book was written about 1840. Apparently Balzac knew that paper produced at the beginning of the 19th century was of lower quality than that made earlier.

The Chinese invented true paper based on the classical definition: "paper is a thin tissue composed of any fibrous material whose individual fibers are first separated by mechanical action and then deposited on a mould suspended in water."

Victor Wolfgang von Hagen wrote in his book, *The Aztec and Maya Papermakers* published in 1944, that great cultural heights have been reached by civilizations without true paper, for instance the Egyptians and Syrians, the Mayas and the Aztecs. "These civilizations developed writing surfaces on which they were able to transmit knowledge from one brain to another, to compile records, to preserve traditions and to develop ideas other than by oral communications. So with paper and writing they freed communication from the limitations of the time-space factor, and by so doing an epochal step in human progress was made." This clearly illustrates the importance of paper for the development of human civilization.

Since the invention of printing technology by Johann Gutenburg, the need for paper has been ever increasing. New inventions have made it possible to satisfy this demand. Before Balzac's novel was written, Carl Wilhelm Scheele had discovered chlorine, which made it possible to bleach colored rags. During the latest decades of the 18th century Nicholas-Louis Robert of France, designed a machine that manufactured paper in an endless web and the brothers Fourdrinier of England improved the machine during the first years of the 19th century.
Papers from the Middle Ages were sized with gelatine in a procedure after the formation of the paper sheet. With the invention of the paper machine a more efficient sizing procedure was necessary, hence rosin sizing was developed.

Rosin was precipitated on the fibers with alum. Alum is acidic and a slow hydrolysis of the cellulose could take place in the paper.

With the new manufacturing techniques and new printing technologies, it was necessary to find substitutes for cotton as papermaking raw material. Finally at the middle of the 19th century the groundwood process was developed and later on the sulphite cooking process. Now wood could be used and no limitations for paper production existed anymore. These early procedures to defibrillate wood fibers by grinding and the acidic sizing procedure caused paper to deteriorate more rapidly than papers from the Middle Ages.

Influence on Permanence

During the first decades of the 20th century acidity was, in the paper science world, understood to have a great influence on paper permanence. Accelerated aging became a test method to predict natural aging and folding endurance was a sensitive evaluation method used. In early scientific works, accelerated aging in a dry climate gave good correlation with natural aging particularly on papers made from cotton. The addition of calcium carbonate to the paper was shown to increase permanence.

It is likely that the hydrolytic deteriorating processes dominate in papers made from pure cellulose, e.g., cotton, thus giving a good correlation between accelerated and natural aging. Results from later studies show, however, that different climates, temperatures and relative humidities, can give different results. It might be that oxidative and cross-linking reactions play a greater role for lignin and hemicelluloses and thus more difficult to predict aging. Natural aging is also dependent on the conditions under which it takes place. No standard climate for natural aging exists.

For many year cotton linters and the addition of small amounts of calcium carbonate were used to make papers with good permanence. This was the situation in the 1980s when the International Standardization Organization through its Technical Committee for Information and Documentation/Physical Keeping of Documents; ISO/TC46/SC10 started its work on a standard for permanent paper.

Standards for Permanent Paper

There are several standards for permanent paper. The two most important ones are ISO 9706:1994 *Information and documentation - Paper for documents - Requirements for permanence*, and ANSI/NISO Z39-48-1992, *American*

National Standard for Permanence of Paper for Publications and Documents in Libraries and Archives. These are very similar in content; only the limiting values of two of the required characteristics, tear resistance and resistance to oxidation, differ slightly.

The ANSI/NISO standard was reaffirmed in 1997 for five years. ISO 9706 underwent a systematic review during 1999, which meant that ISO asked all members of ISO/TC 46/SC 10 if the standard needs revision or if it can be confirmed for another five years. The standard is based on the present state of knowledge and as long as new scientific results on permanence have not been proved the standard should not be revised. A decision was made at the ISO/TC 46/SC 10 meeting in May 1999 to uphold the excisting parallelity between ANSI/NISO Z39-48 and ISO 9706 also in the future.

During the development of ISO 9706, experts from libraries, archives and the paper industry collaborated together in the working group. We discussed the current needs and possibilities and we studied the paper process and the situation at the archives. All parties got an understanding of each other's problems and difficulties. As papermakers we understood that our cultural heritage was at stake due to faulty papermaking procedures. We then had better procedures, neutral systems with calcium carbonate as filler, and were able to produce paper with high permanence without increasing costs.

The Impact of Lignin on Permanence

The discussion now is whether lignin is detrimental or not. Accelerated aging is often used for studies of permanence and is claimed to prove that papers containing lignin show very little deterioration. Some scientists even claim that lignin might be a benefit to permanence. Still we know very little about the reactions taking place in paper during aging, both during natural aging and accelerated aging, and we do not know how these reactions correlate.

When the working group was in action solutions were reached as a result of understanding each other's problems. We based our decisions on mutual respect and as papermakers we found that the fear for lignin-containing papers was very strong among the experts from archives and libraries. They had numerous experiences of deteriorated material which had to be restored at high costs. We as papermakers also had to take our repsonsibility for preserving our cultural heritage. We had the knowledge to produce paper with high permanence, and there were reasons to take every precaution and exclude material that we knew too little about.

We know that
- lignin is easily oxidized
- lignin causes severe color change
- lignin-containing papers discolor other papers in contact with them.

However, ISO 9706 does not state any limit for lignin content. Instead, the Standard has a limit in Kappa number, a figure that expresses the material's sensitivity to oxidation. The logic was , if the paper is sensitive to oxidation, it is likely to oxidize over time and thus be unstable over long periods.

Research Programmes on Permanence

The American Society of Testing and Materials and its Institute for Standards Research is engaged in a multi-year research programme to create scientifically sound methods for the predication of the life expectancy of printing and writing papers. Its goal is to expand the understanding of fundamental mechanisms of paper aging and to develop accelerated aging test methods that correlate well with natural aging results. To ensure maximum reproducibility, special papers were made for this purpose. They cover a wide range of different compositions. These papers are aged with different methods and also naturally aged at different locations. ASTM/ISR claims that the goals will be reached with good probability.

The Pulp and Paper Research Institute of Canada has just completed a research project where they have tested handsheets and commercial papers which are acid and neutral, wood-free and wood-containing. The paper samples have been aged at 80°C and 65% relative humidity for up to 50 days. They show that zero-span and average degree of polymerization change very little neutral papers independent of lignin content. (Zero-span is a test method for fiber strength and degree of polymerization measures the chemical deterioration of cellulose.) However the loss of brightness was more pronounced for samples with high lignin content.

An ISO standard under development, ISO/CD 16559 *Information and Documentation - Archival Board - Migration* Test is intended for testing of boards to be used for protection of archival material. The board to be tested is placed adjacent to a blotting paper of pure cellulose. The change of brightness of the blotting paper is measured. We have used this method on papers of different quality and found the following results. Papers made of 100% chemical pulp which have low Kappa numbers show low discoloration. Acidic papers discolor more. Papers containing mechanical fibers also discolor more while acidic and buffered more than neutral papers. This is the case for most papers. Some experts claim that this discoloration might also decrease strength. This method is not suitable for measuring strength properties.

Conclusions

It is not just a question of how lignin influences permanence. Modern pulp and paper making uses additives to reach the required characteristics and to perform well in the process. Their effect on permanence must also be taken into consideration. For instance additives with high amounts of double bonds are easily oxidized and will increase the Kappa number. There are still many questions to be answered on what influences permanence of paper. As was said before we can not take the risk to jeopardize our cultural heritage and allow material that we know too little about in archives and libraries. After all there is enough paper in the world to fullfil the requirements of ISO 9706. Even if ongoing research programmes will attempt to answer some questions other questions will remain. We need to see significant differences between the naturally aged papers before we can change the requirements of permanence.

The future of ISO 9706 as a standard with relevant requirements for permanence depends on the number of organizations supporting its existence. That can be accomplished by joining ISO/TC46 through your national standardization organization as a P-member or by an A-liaison member such as IFLA.

Inga-Lisa Svensson, Mo & Domsjö AB, Örnsköldsvik, Sweden and
Ylwa Alwarsdotter, Stora Fine Paper AB, Nymölla, Sweden
(present address AssiDomän AB, Dynäs, Sweden)

[The paper by Ms Svensson and Ms Alwarsdotter was delivered during the 64th IFLA General Conference, Amsterdam, Netherlands, 16-21 August 1998.]

Beatrix Kastaly

Permanent Paper and the Brittle Book Problem in Hungary

Introduction

Outside of libraries and archives it is not very widely known yet that the books, journals, newspapers, posters, maps and other publications and certain parts of the manuscript documents which have been produced on paper since the 1860s and 1870s are threatened by gradual but sure self-destruction. The common characteristic of these papers is that their acid content is relatively significant (their pH value is between 3 and 5). This can be attributed to the fact that the sizing of the pulp has been carried out in an acid medium since the beginning of the last century. If the paper contains a major quantity of mechanical woodpulp (since the mid-19th century), these two factors together cause a high degree of brittleness. Brittleness of paper means that paper can not withstand one double fold but breaks to pieces.

Surveys which have been carried out in different libraries in the world show that there are enormous quantities of already brittle books, newspapers and other printed and manuscript documents both in Europe, America and Asia. In the USA there were 80 million, and in Germany (in the Western part only) 30 million books. At the National Széchényi Library, the National Library of Hungary, the paper is brittle in 10% of the books, about 230,000 volumes. Besides the books, there are 500,000 theatre bills, most of them acid and/or brittle. Naturally there are many other types of printed and manuscript material also on papers which are acid and in a more or less brittle state.

Among them the most significant one is the newspaper collection which contains about 300,000 volumes of newspapers and journals. The quantity of newspapers separately can not be determined exactly. In spite of that in 1888 a separate division was created inside the library as a Newspaper Library, and later the journals were added to it.

In Hungary newspaper preservation as such is a task which falls mostly to the National Library. In other libraries those newspapers which are to be retained permanently will be bound sooner or later and stored in various environmental conditions. Approximately 70% of the old pre-1952 newspapers of the nation can be found only in the National Library in relative completeness. But the National Library had never had sufficient resources for properly storing and binding all its newspapers. Besides the inherent acidity and brittleness of the paper, this was the other reason why considerable amounts in the '60s were in poor condition; they were very brittle, crumbling, yellow or even brown.

Preservation Microfilming

Using the brittle, printed materials is no longer possible and that is why libraries do their best to transfer the content of these documents to other formats and the surrogate copies can then be consulted.

To preserve the information content of the newspapers as much as possible it was decided to microfilm all the Hungarica newspapers of the National Library. The financial, technical and personnel necessary for this work have been provided by the government. Since 1969, the retrospective microfilming of newspapers has been in progress and about one million pages have been microfilmed annually.

Before microfilming, smaller or greater repairs or full conservation have to be performed on the old newspapers to secure the best legibility possible. When the paper is very brittle and crumbling we deacidify and strengthen it. The latter is done by lamination with polyethylene and Japanese tissue.

The archival quality master negatives have been preserved in an air-conditioned archive at 15-16°C and 30-40% RH. Second negatives, however, have not been made. The positive films are kept in the storerooms of the newspapers. The originals - if their positive film copy is available - may be consulted in exceptional cases only. After being microfilmed, the original newspapers are retained at the National Library because most of the old newspapers can only be found here, and, in many cases, in one copy only. The original newspapers, if they are unbound, are placed in custom-made corrugated boxes lined with alkaline paper. This is also the preservation method applied for the archival copies of the current newspapers. The second copies of the current newspapers are to be bound because they may be consulted until they have been microfilmed.

The newspaper microfilms are regularly recorded and published in registers at the national library. From these registers other libraries can order microfilms against payment to complete or preserve their newspaper holdings. The microfilms made at the National Library are as complete as possible, because the titles which are not complete in the National Library are completed with the missing parts from other libraries. The National Library has also microfilmed Hungarica newspapers in libraries of some of the neighboring countries (Austria, Slovakia, the Czech Republic, Serbia and Croatia).

In 1997 a new project was launched at the National Library: the microfilming of certain brittle books. The first criterium of selection for microfilming is use. After the first consultation a brittle book is placed in a phase box which is labelled and the date of consultation is noted on it. The second use will also be noted and then, after the third consultation, the book will be microfilmed. When the positive microfilm is available, the label on the box says that "this book may be consulted through microfilm only". If the paper of the book is extremely brittle it will be microfilmed before or after the first consultation.

Deacidification and Strengthening

The retrospective microfilming of newspapers will end in a few years. The last several years of some current newspapers (those which originate from before 1952) have been also microfilmed. The microfilming of other current newspapers will follow the retrospective microfilming. Then the repair work will decrease to a minimum, and thus the task of the conservators will change. They will deacidify and strengthen the paper of the most valuable and unique newspapers because the national library wants to retain them permanently. We have not yet determined the mass treatment by which these aims would be achieved. The paper of most of our old newspapers is much too weak and brittle; that is why impregnation with an adhesive only is not sufficient for them. Deacidification and strengthening by hand is highly time-consuming.

Acid-free and/or Permanent Paper

The experience of the last 120-130 years led to the recognition that for the future the only good and preventive solution is if non-acid paper is produced from pure cellulose with an alkaline reserve for archival purposes.

In Hungarian paper mills the first trials for producing paper in neutral medium using a synthetic sizing agent and calcium carbonate filler were carried out between 1975 and 1980, but at that time the introduction of this technology for the production of writing and printing paper was prevented by the instability of the sizing dispersion and uneconomic prices. After initial attempts, the first big breakthrough occurred in 1984 when one of the paper machines in the Szolnok paper mill was converted to the use of acid-free materials. This conversion was necessary because the waste products which formed on the coating machine, which used calcium carbonate pigment, could not be recycled since the medium was acid. Conversion meant that not only was aluminium sulphate no longer used, but that a synthetic sizing agent was added which brought changes throughout the whole technology of papermaking. The successful conversion in Szolnok, the increasing price of sizing agents based on pine resin (which needs the acidic medium), the reasonable price and ever-increasing quality and quantity of fillers based on Hungarian carbonates, convinced the other mills too. The percentage of acid-free writing and printing paper produced in Hungary is a very clear indication of the tendency: from 10% in 1984, 30% in 1986, over 60% in 1990 and 100% by today.

In the 1980s the conservation research group of the national library performed many experiments together with a papermill and the Paper Research Institute to produce a lignin- and acid-free, thin but durable and permanent paper with a good opacity. The national library planned to copy the deposit copies of the newly published newspapers onto this paper in order to reduce the volume of newspapers needing conservation in the future. By the early '90s we succeeded in formulating the suitable composition, but in the last years the national library had no financial possibility to get a thin paper of great mechanical strength produced (which should be free of groundwood and should contain cotton- and pine-pulps) and to purchase a photocopy machine of large size suitable for copying newspapers.

Meanwhile the technology of the manufacturing of the imported newsprint paper used in Hungary has also changed. The acid medium in which sizing was previously made has been converted to a neutral or an alkaline one and this made possible the use of calcium carbonate filler. Thus these newsprint papers are no longer acid but slightly alkaline, and obviously do not deteriorate so fast as the acid one. Because of their poor fiber composition, their mechanical strength naturally is not great enough, but they preserve their original strength for a longer time.

Similarly to the producers of newsprint paper, many of the manufacturers of writing and printing papers have converted their technology from sizing in acid medium to sizing in neutral or alkaline (one in Western and one in Central Europe). This made it possible to use an alkaline filler, calcium carbonate, instead of clay, which is a neutral one without a positive impact for the permanence of paper. During the second half of the '80s, the cost of carbonates from which a better ratio of whiteness in paper could be achived decreased, thus making the production of acid-free paper more economical. This was important because price is the dominant factor in the industry, not permanence.

The quantity of acid-free paper made in Hungary is not equal to the quantity actually used, taking import and export into account. As a consequence of the complete liberalization of the import policy into Hungary since 1989-1990, vast quantities of printing paper have been imported and numerous new publishers and printing offices often show preference for foreign paper because of its good quality and relatively low price.

Knowing the big change in the production of non-acid printing papers in Hungary between 1986 and 1996 and the fact that a great quantity of paper was imported from Western, Central and Northern Europe for the books which were published in Hungary during the last ten years, one could assume that the prevailing role of acidic book paper has ceased. To gain a clear view on this question we have tested the acidity/alkalinity and the presence of lignin in the paper of those books which got to the national library as deposit copies between 1986 and 1996. By a random but statistically relevant sampling 450 books printed on non-coated paper were chosen and tested.

The ratio of acid-free papers used for the printing of books seemed to be stabilized around 85% in Hungary during the last five years. This proves that sizing in neutral or alkaline media and the use of calcium carbonate as filler are spreading steadily in the European papermaking technology, and that the use of neutral or alkaline printing papers is already predominant in Hungary.

In 1993 and 1994 the Research Institute for the Paper Industry tested 10 different (printing, photocopying and preservation) papers produced by three Hungarian paper mills to establish whether these papers met the requirements of the ISO 9706 standard. This testing was initiated by the National Archives and the National Library. All papers met the requirements but the mills have not attached great importance to this because they have not mentioned the permanence of their papers in the description of their products. Thus the publishers and printing offices cannot get information on it and they could not deliberately apply these acid-free or often permanent papers even if they wanted to. And in their publications they cannot mention that "this paper meets the requirements of the ... standard". That is why I think that libraries and library organizations should make further efforts to ensure that quality (including permanence) of the paper be indicated in the product descriptions of paper mills. The name, quality and origin of the paper, together with the exact name of the manufacturer, should also be indicated in publications. This would provide a base for estimating the life expectancy of each publication, particularly if the aging properties of the paper used are known.

References

1. Kastaly, Beatrix. "How Hungary Has Tackled the Brittle Paper Issue". *International Preservation News*. 16:6-8(January 1998).
2. Kastaly, Beatrix. Időálló hazai nyomópapírok. (Permanent printing papers in Hungary) *Magyar Grafika*. 3:43-47(1995)

3. Kastaly, Beatrix. "The Composition of Permanent Papers" *in Proceedings of the Conference on Book and Paper Conservation, Budapest 4-7 September 1990.* Budapest, 1992.
4. Völgyi, Péter. "Acid-free Papermaking in Hungary" *in Proceedings of the Conference on Book and Paper Conservation, Budapest 4-7 September 1990.* Budapest, 1992.
5. Kastaly, Beatrix. "Newspaper Preservation in Hungary" *in Newspaper Preservation and Access. Proceedings of the Symposium held in London, August 12-15, 1987.* Vol. I-II. K.G. Saur. München-New York-London-Paris, 1988.

Beatrix Kastaly
Newspaper Preservation Department,
National Széchényi Library,
Budapest, Hungary

[Ms Kastaly's paper was presented during the 64th IFLA General Conference, Amsterdam, Netherlands, 16-21 August 1998.]

Rujaya Abhakorn

The Making of Oral History in Thailand

In Thailand, memory about the past has been recorded in written manuscripts through an oral tradition that was usually limited to political dynastic events, history of Buddhism and Buddhist relics, and local history, which again was usually confined to the history of the ruling family or local Buddhism, although we could also sometimes find legends and myths. These were periodically recopied by several people for their own reasons with little addition. Keeping a record of one's own thoughts and activities in the form of a diary has hardly ever been practiced. In fact, political leaders and their family members and close associates usually kept silent about their experiences and let them die with them.

The idea of recording people's versions of their lives or certain episodes in their lives is therefore of a very recent origin in Thailand. The reason for this is not the lack of modern technology. It is the unwillingness to reveal the facts and be responsible for the consequences that keeps the practice of recording the present in order to fill the past somewhat a novelty.

Interest in history as a serious academic subject as well as an intellectual tool in the understanding of social change and political development was at its height in the early 1970s and seemed to stimulate the making of oral history. The Historical Society of Thailand was founded by a group of university history teachers and students in 1978. Before that, the study and use of history was dominated by the state in order to promote national consciousness. After the so-called "Students Revolution" of 1973 in which the military regime was overthrown by popular demonstrations, there were demands for "the people's history" to replace the history of the state and the ruling class. The installation of an elected government also revived an interest in the history of democracy in Thailand that began in 1932 by a group of government officials who forced the royal government to introduce a constitution and parliamentary democracy.

This article is based on a rough survey, with the kind assistance of Nakharin Mektrairat and Warunee Osatharom of Thammasat University, of "oral history projects" conducted since 1976 as well as publications that used oral interviews. The result shows that a state agency, the National Archives, and academic historians have played the most active roles in the making of oral history in the modern era. There appear to be three types of oral history, all of which are political in nature, but reflecting three different concerns: the history of the state, the history of the democratic movement and the history of the people.

The National Archives and Oral History

The National Archives in Thailand was officially established to collect official documents generated in the course of their routine duties by all the bureaucratic agencies in the country. As part of its responsibilities, the National Archives collected tapes of important royal ceremonies, parliamentary debates, and political campaign speeches, all of which took place in Bangkok. It was only after two important political events of 14 October 1973 and the political violence of 5 October 1976, that the Archival Section of the National Archives initiated a project called "Talking about Old Times" in 1976 in which it interviewed six persons of different statuses and importance. The most famous was M.R. Kukrit Pramoj, a royalist and former prime minister best known for his multi-talents as writer, classical dancer, historian, and political skills, who was at the height of his career. Another royalist interviewed was Princess Poonpismai Diskul, a daughter of Prince Damrong Rajanuphap, who was a close adviser and brother of King Chulalongkorn. The Princess reminisced about life at court, her father and his political downfall after the coup of 1932, and her personal interests, particularly in Buddhism. Three other well-known writers also talked about their lives and interests. Khun Wichit Matra, another man of letters and composer, gave an account of life in Bangkok at the beginning of the 20th century. Sathit Semanin, a journalist and writer talked about political changes as seen from the media's angle. Another old-time journalist, Phayom Rotchanawiphat, also talked about his life in the early 20th century. The last person recorded under this project was a man of a completely different nature, a man remembered today as the leader of a violent group of right-wing political activists who were involved in the clashes of 6 October 1976 at Thammasat University. Colonel Sudsai Hasadin was the leader of the Red Guard anti-communist para-military group consisting mainly of young students from vocational schools who set out to physically oppose university students suspected of being communist sympathizers.

"Talking about Old Times" was not a particularly well-conceived project. There was no clear objective or theme and, with the exception of Colonel Sudsai, all of those interviewed were writers who had already put on paper their thoughts and experiences. The project, by recording their voices, made them more "real" for future listeners and historians, without adding much more to what was already known from written sources.

In 1977, this project was reorganized to reflect the academic "oral history" approach. Questionnaires were prepared and preliminary researches made. Unfortunately, as it turned out, only three persons were interviewed, two of whom, Khun Phra Sucharit Suda, and Khun Phra Adisai Sawamiphak, were courtiers in the reign of King Rama VI (1910-1919). The third person, Rabin Bunnag, was a professional photographer of social life. His collection of photographs later became part the of National Archives Photograph Section.

Since then, the National Archives has frozen its oral history project, apparently for the lack of personnel and funding. Given the nature of its governing agency, the Fine Arts Department of the Ministry of Education, which liked to be self-sufficient without seeking cooperation from the universities, it is not surprising that the project was not sustainable.

Academic Oral History

Research using oral history as a technique in gathering data in addition to the information already available in official publications and newspapers was conducted in Thai universities by three main groups: political economists, political scientists and historians. All of them are best described as contemporary political history. Five works are cited here.

The work by Charnwit Kasetsiri[1] and others is essentially a history of Thammasat University, emphasizing the point that the University's history was intertwined with political events and the political life of Thailand. The reasons for this were its connection with its founder, Pridi Phanomyong and the commitments of its students to democratic ideals. Researchers for this work were teachers and students of Thai political history; their investigation was extensive, using official and personal records, newspapers and secondary sources more than personal interviews of former teachers, students and administrators. The number of those interviewed (38) was not extensive and could not include two very important people, Pridi Phanomyong the University founder who passed away in Paris a few weeks before an arranged meeting could take place, and the late Duean Bunnag who was in charge of the University's administration during Pridi's political exile in the 1950s. As the researchers' main theme was how the university's moral and political ideals survived in the midst of political authoritarianism, the voices of the "radical" elements of Thammasat University were heard and given more space than their opponents in the entire work.Nevertheless, this history shows how a university history should be presented as part of the social and political life of the country, and not just an autonomous educational institution. It also belongs to a growing field of the history of the Thai democratic movement, which at the moment is documentary-based with either a journalistic or populistic approach.

Kanok Wongtrangan's work on *Politics in the House of Representatives*[2] concentrated on the working mechanics of the Thai House of Representatives, which also included the politics of elections. In spite of the aim at studying the actors, that is the members of the House of Representatives, only 13 MPs were interviewed, albeit some were important members, such as M.R. Seni Pramoj, a former Prime Minister; Banharn Silpaacha, who later became one; and Sawat Khamprakop, a veteran MP. Kanok tended to show the usefulness of his interviewees whose opinions on electioneering, the roles of the poltical parties, the legislative process and the conduct of parlimentarians support his own theoretical framework. There were no stunning revelations on political secrets or backroom dramas that one would like to see in political history since this work was conducted as a political scientist's research.

Yot's work[3] on the other hand, focused on individual politicians or powerful figures whom he interviewed one by one. They were M.R. Seni Pramoj; Field Marshal Thanom Kittikachorn, a "dictator" whose government fell in 1973; Thanin Kraiwichien, a legal expert and judge who headed a right-wing government after the chaos of 1976 only to be ousted in a military coup 377 days later; and Boonchu Rojanasathian, a banker who turned politician and became popularly known as an "Economic Czar" for his expertise in economic affairs. In spite of the small number of those interviewed, Yot managed to dig into their personal thoughts and obtained new data on some of the political intrigues that are essential parts of Thai political history. He let his informants "present themselves" as they were, and in the last three chapters in his book he analyzed their opinions on his chosen topics of the concept of power, leadership and the Thai power structure. His research met the expectations that oral history should provide us with useful new data gained though interviews as well as an indication of how they relate to wider issues of interest.

The economic condition of the people seems to be the focus of the Political Economy Group of "left-wing" economists at Chulalongkorn University. Their leader, Professor Chatthip Natsupha, was behind what is probably the largest oral history project undertaken so far in Thailand. The result is a surprisingly small pocket book[4] on the village history of the whole country divided into four regions, the north, northeast, central and south. A total of 178 villagers were interviewed. The information gained helped him to build his thesis that from the 15th century to 1855, the date of the Bowring Treaties that forced open Thai economy to free trade, the Thai village was economically self-sufficient. After 1855, the central plain economy became a market economy, while other regions still maintained their self-sufficiency. This thesis in fact was based on documentary study prior to this research and the oral history investigation prompted Chatthip to show the differences between the regions. The oral information is well integrated into the thesis. It would be useful for other researchers if some of the transcripts are available in full so that alternative interpretations could be made.

The work of Phasuk Phongphaichit, a member of this group, could also be marginally classified as oral history. *Underground Economy and Public Policy in Thailand*[5] touched on the dark aspect of contemporary politics and economy: the illicit economic activities that linked politicians with business. The nature of the topic made it unwise to reveal the names of the informants. The research result therefore contains no name of the persons interviewed, but made headlines because of the intriguing nature of the topic.

A recent contribution on the making of oral history is a thesis by Chaiwat Suphadiloklak[6] of Thammasat University who worked on the economic history of the northern Thai province of Lampang in the early 20th century. Altogether 54 people were interviewed giving a good picture of the urban economy of this city. Although it produces no new thesis, it answers some of the questions related to the issue of the "formation of the capitalist class" that interest the political economy school.

Conclusion

Oral history in Thailand is used in conjunction with the general techniques of historical research rather than being conducted autonomously. From the academic historian's point of view, this is how it should be done. The problem is that the researcher's interests are at present highly selective and new topics only emerge slowly. Meanwhile, people with useful memory pass away, taking with them historical evidence. Libraries and archives could perform a useful task here, provided that they also do their history homework and are in tune with the information need of their communities.

References

1. Charnwit Kasetsiri. Samnak nan Thammasat lae karnmuang karnmuang pho so 2477-2511 (That School Thammasat and Political Sciences 1934-1968). Bangkok: Dokya Press, 1992.

2. Kanok Wongtrangan. Kan muang nai sapha phuthaen ratsadorn (Politics in the House of Representatives). Bangkok: Chulalongkorn University Press, 1987.

3. Yot Santasombat. Amnat, bukkhalikkaphap lae phunam karnmuang Thai (Power, Personality and Thai Political Leaders) Bangkok: Thammasat University Press, 1990.

4. Chatthip Natsupha. Setthakit muban Thai nai adeet (Thai Village Economy in the Past.). Bangkok: Sangsan Press, 1984.

5. Phasuk Phongphaichit et al. Karn prachum raingan phon karn wichai ruang Setthakit nok kotmai lae nayobai satharana nai prathet Thai (Seminar Report on Illicit Economy and Public Policy in Thailand). Bangkok: Chulalongkorn University Political Economy Center, 1996.

6. Chaiwat Supphadiloklak. Pho kha kap kan phatthnakan setthakit: Lampang pho so 2459-2512 (Merchants and Economic Development: Lampang 1916-1972). MA Thesis, Faculty of Political Science, Thammasat University, 1999.

Rujaya Abhakorn
Department of History
Chaing Mai University
Thailand

[Mr Abhakorn's paper was presented at the 65th IFLA Council and General Conference, Thailand, 20-28 August 1999.]

Colin Webb

Safeguarding the Oral Heritage in Australia

Introduction

Safeguarding the oral heritage in Australia is more than a matter of building and preserving collections. The rich oral heritage of this country has been nourished by thousands of years of oral culture, and enriched by one of the most diverse cultural and ethnic mixes in the world. It is still hard to see whether this heritage is being further enriched or impoverished by recurring waves of technology that seem to diminish person-to-person interaction.

Indeed Australians are among the world's most enthusiastic takers-up of new communications technologies. True believers are inclined to argue at length about what is oral history, folkore, ethnomusicology, or published sound. This paper will take a broad and perhaps superficial approach that recognizes as oral heritage such diverse manifestations as: historic recordings of indigenous language speakers, former politicians discussing their terms in office, migration experiences, indigenous gumleaf players, old folk remembering how things used to be, unemployed young people talking about how it is right now, collections of interviews around particular events or trends loosely described as social history, well researched and structured autobiographical interviews with prominent individuals, and essentially non-commercial recordings documenting songs, stories, music. Under the banner of oral history and folklore, I will focus on how well these are documented and preserved.

A Network of Folk Revival Organizations

"Collecting" - recording oral heritage - has been quite actively pursued. The Oral History Association has branches in most states, publishes an annual journal and organizes a biennial national conference. There are strong personal links between the Association and many of the institutions involved in active collecting, storing and preserving material.

On the folklore front, the existence of a strong network of folk revival organizations does not accurately reflect the level of folklore collecting activity, which has depended on the extraordinary efforts of a relatively few individuals, often supported by institutions and grants but basically defining and organizing their own collecting effort, usually within their own areas of interest.

At Least 500 Collections Have Been Indexed

In terms of safeguarding collections two major initiatives over the past decade stand out. In 1986 the Commonwealth government set up a Committee of Inquiry into Folklife in Australia. Its Report, released in 1987, was an attempt to provide some direction within a series of broad management proposals, including the establishment of an Australian Folklife Centre "to provide a national focus for action to record, safeguard, and promote Australia's heritage of folklife". The Report proposed a close working relationship between this Centre and existing national institutions which would house and preserve a National Collection of Australian Folklife. Those key recommendations of the Committee were not taken up, but the Inquiry, which attracted almost 250 substantial written submissions, did help focus and stimulate the efforts of a number of national institutions and raised the profile of folklife collecting.

In 1992, Australian libraries held a conference in Canberra entitled "Towards Federation 2001: Linking Australians and their Heritage". One of the conference resolutions was that a national directory of oral history and folklore collections should be compiled. After some years' work by a committee with representatives from all states and territories the directory was released in draft form. It is not exhaustive (there are almost certainly other collections in private hands that have been missed) but it will still be an extraordinarily useful document for looking at the state of oral heritage in Australia.

The Australian Oral History Directory lists some 500 collections held around the country, varying in size from more than 30,000 hours in the National Library of Australia (NLA), down to half a dozen collections comprising just one tape (not necessarily a true indication of importance!). Although there are at least 11 collections holding more than 1,000 hours of material, there are a lot of very small collections: 40% of entries are for collections containing 20 or fewer items, while more than 20% contain 10 or less.

The directory also tells us a lot about where material is held, though less about its condition and how well collections are stored and managed. National institutions with significant holdings include the NLA, Australian Institute for Aboriginal and Torres Strait Islander Studies, National Film and Sound Archive, Australian Broadcasting Commission, Australian War Memorial, National Museum of Australia, National Maritime Museum, and Australian Archives. Most of these hold material of national significance within a particular collecting mandate.

Aboriginal Groups Have Set Up Projects

However, many oral heritage materials are of regional or local significance so it is not surprising that some of the largest collections are held by State libraries and State archives services, while more than 200 entries are for collections held by local government bodies (mainly public libraries) or volunteer-based local history societies. There are smaller but still significant holdings in the hands of organizations like schools, religious bodies, professional and occupational associations, companies, government departments, ethnic communities, community theatres, sporting associations and recreational groups. Many of these are using oral history as a tool to document their own development.

The oral heritage of indigenous peoples has been a research focus for many decades, but in recent years a number of Aboriginal groups have set up their own exciting projects documenting, reclaiming, and in some cases returning their oral heritage to their communities.

Academic institutions have played a special role. At least 26 universities are listed in the Directory; only two of these appear to hold exclusively corporate archives. Largely due to the research focus of individuals working in anthropology, history, music and English departments, a number of very important collections have been established in university libraries, archives, and faculties. These include the Australian Children's Folklore Collection at the University of Melbourne, the Western Victoria Oral History Project at Deakin University, the Archive of Australian Judaica at the University of Sydney, and the Western Australian Folklore Archive at the Curtin University of Technology. There are currently few programmes developing the disciplines of studying this material.

Approximately 60 collections listed in the Directory are privately held. Most of these are small, but some are significant in content or size. Some are simply interesting, such as the 6 oral history interviews that constitute the Courtship and Dating Collection held by a private collector in Adelaide.

Most Recordings Date Back to the Late 1940s

Much of the material listed in the Directory was collected in the 1980s and '90s, and many projects are ongoing. The earliest oral heritage recordings include a 1928 collection of Aboriginal material held by the South Australian Museum Anthropology Department, and 1939 recordings held by NLA. Most of what we would recognize as oral history and folklore recording has happened since the introduction of the portable tape recorder following its adoption by historians in the late 1940s.

So, Australia's recorded oral heritage is diverse in content, collected in truly diverse circumstances at different times, with a range of expectations and expertise, in a range of formats and standards. Some material has national significance, some mainly regional, local, or family value.

While this diversity has many positives, it means that the safeguarding of that heritage material is very problematic. The Directory did not ask about threats and problems (with hindsight it could have told us much more about preservation needs than it does) but we can draw some inferences. And we do know that there are diverse approaches to preservation, often the subject of debate and disagreement about what is needed.

DAT: Higher Quality but Less Stable Format

Most of the materials used to document oral heritage are unstable by nature, subject to the deterioration of carriers such as cellulose acetate and PVC tapes and polyurethane binders. Their chemical and physical instability is exacerbated by unsuitable storage conditions such as high or fluctuating humidity, high temperatures, polluted air and exposure to magnetic fields. Field collecting has often been done in just such circumstances.

The recordings are machine-readable. When they fail, one cannot hold them up to the light to recover information. The easiest to use, least expensive and most popular recording formats such as audio cassettes, are not particularly robust and are easily damaged by use and more quickly degraded by adverse storage conditions. Even for professional grade reel-to-reel tapes recovery methods (such as baking unplayable items) are difficult to control, expensive and risky.

Technological change has always been a potential problem for sound recordings but it is becoming a pressing threat. It has introduced higher quality but less stable formats such as DAT (digital audio tape), and the rate of change is bringing forward the time when recordings must be copied even if they are in excellent condition. There have been a number of responses to these challenges, including safe storage, copying, transcription, and publishing.

Safe Storage and Copying Are Insured by State Institutions

Many people are relying on storage in suitable conditions either in their own facilities or by transferring to repositories in State libraries and other institutions. This seems to be worth doing just to improve security against theft or disaster. It is most useful where conditions can be maintained that will significantly slow down the rate of deterioration. Conditions need to be cool, dry, stable and clean (for example, in line with the 1995 recommendations of John van Bogart of the US National Media Lab). Even though safe storage buys time and so can be considered necessary for preservation, it does not by itself resolve the problems of technological change so it is almost certainly not sufficient.

The most widely accepted standard for sound archiving is to copy material, producing a preservation master (to be put away and only used to migrate to a preservation master in another format), a back-up copy, and a user copy. Sound archives try to ensure that they use high quality materials and spread their risk by using different types of carrier for preservation and back-up copies.

Increasingly, as the commercial market for analogue audio technology shrinks, digital technology is being used to make the preservation copy (often on Recordable-CD), providing a carrier that is expected to outlive the technology needed to read it, and a format that can be copied without data loss at faster than real time when migration is necessary. Some institutions, including NLA, are still backing up their digital copy with an analogue reel-to-reel tape; in line with current International Association of Sound and Audiovisual Archives (IASAVA) Technical Committee recommendations. Even where collection managers are not able to provide this level of archiving many still look to some kind of copying to reduce the risk of loss associated with use.

Transcription and Publications Are other Preservation Alternatives

Converting the information content of a sound recording to a written form is widely used to provide a level of access and to document the recording in case of loss. The adequacy of transcripts as a preservation measure depends on the purposes of the collection: in many cases the recorded sound is considered important, and the transcript a pale reflection. However, where the sound recording is unlikely to survive a verbatim transcript may be the only feasible preservation path.

Transcription is an expensive process, unless it can be done by volunteers. In the not-too-distant future it may be possible to generate transcripts automatically from sound recordings using voice recognition software; it is already possible to link indexing point in digital sound files with key indexing points in summaries. For larger institutions able to access this technology, the days of the verbatim transcript as a standard oral history tool may be numbered. On the other hand, digitized transcriptions themselves can provide a level of networked access that we may not be able to achieve with sound recordings for some time.

Few Collections Are Managed with an Integrated Archiving Plan

Sixty of the smaller collections in the Directory indicate that their recorded material has been or will be used in publications or in unpublished university theses. Of course, many of the collections in larger institutions are also drawn on for published research. This may amount to a kind of representative preservation for part of their intellectual content, which may be adequate in some cases (although most collectors and curators are still keen to maintain access to the primary source material).

Just how widely and how well these and other preservation approaches are being used is hard to determine. Until we ask the right questions we will not know. Anecdotal evidence suggests that few collections are being managed with an integrated archiving plan incorporating reasonably stable materials, safe storage, reliable back-ups, and migration to deal with technological change. Many more are using transcription and/or publication, but even then almost half of the entries in the Directory indicate either no or very few transcripts have been made.

Cooperative Preservation Action Is Certainly the Key

Improving the situation will be challenging. Beyond letting material become unusable we know there are no easy solutions, especially for such a diverse and dispersed national collections (if such a concept is even appropriate). Full-scale sound archiving is expensive and few institutions have spare resources to deal actively with material outside their own collections.

As with other preservation challenges, we know that education, information, advice, guidelines and standards can help. (Edgar Waters' booklet mentioned in the references is a good example). But even with good guidelines and advice, resource issues still seem critical for such technology dependant material. In such a context the very worthwhile objective of supporting local control and care of local materials is itself a powerful constraint.

On the other hand, we have had very good experience with cooperative preservation action in other fields. It worked for "The Last Film Search" project locating cellulose nitrate films before they turned to dust or flame, and it is currently working for NPLAN, the National Plan for Australian Newspapers, which has brought all State libraries and the NLA together to locate and preserve copies of all known Australian newspapers. There has been talk of a National Serials Plan along the same lines, and similar collaboration will be needed for the preservation of digital information.

So perhaps there is room to be optimistic about cooperative action for at risk oral heritage materials. Already there are some links between institutions, some assistance provided and preservation responsibilities identified. If we are to take further action, we will need to follow up on the information our Oral History Directory gives us; we will need to talk to each other more, and in ways that don't push buttons of defensiveness. And we will need to find ways into a Pandora's box of expectations that we can cope with.

Note: The author acknowledges the assistance of Kevin Bradley (Sound Preservation) and National Library of Australia, and collection managers in a number of other institutions, in preparing this article. The views expressed, however, are his own.

References

1. Committee of Inquiry into Folklife in Australia. *Folklife: Our Living Heritage*. Canberra, AGPS, 1987.
2. IASAVA Technical Committee, Annual Conference, Perugia, August/September 1996. *Minutes of Working Meeting*, unpublished.
3. Van Bogart, John. *Magnetic Tape Storage and Handling: A Guide for Libraries and Archives*. St. Paul: Commission on Preservation and Access & National Media Laboratory,1995.
4. Waters, Edgar. *Guidelines for Audio and Audiovisual Recording in the South Pacific*. Canberra: National Library of Australia, 1995. Available online at URL: <http://www/nla.gov.au.an/niac/watersla.html>

Colin Webb
Manager of Information Preservation
National Library of Australia
Canberra, Australia

[Mr Webb's article was originally published in *International Preservation News* 14 (May 1997).]

Rujaya Abhakorn

Towards A Collective Memory of Mainland Southeast Asia: Field Preservation of Traditional Manuscripts in Thailand, Laos and Myanmar

Introduction

Mainland Southeast Asia comprises Myanmar, Thailand, Laos, Cambodia, Vietnam and peninsular Malaysia. These national designations are of a very recent origin, tracing back to the late 19th century when the two imperialist powers, France and Great Britain, divided up the traditional kingdoms and principalities of Southeast Asia among themselves. These polities had emerged from several thousand years of cultural experience that taught the inhabitants of the hills and river valleys how to coexist with nature and other people peacefully. The rivalries, exploitations and wars are important parts of their memory as well as the religious bonds and marital ties among the different groups of Mons, Khmers, Thais, Burmese, and Vietnamese. The diverse cultural practices have common ground in the respect for the external life forces and the elders, the art of living with nature and with other peoples, regardless of the ethnic or language differences. The cultural practices of Theravada Buddhism in Myanmar, Thailand, Laos and Cambodia are perhaps the most visible manifestation of regional cohesion. The formation of national ideologies and the encroachment of Western values and life-styles have led to the neglect and destruction of this classical Southeast Asian common ground. In many cases, what is left can only be found in paper or palm-leaf documents. Unfortunately, these too are also under threat from neglect or willful destruction by all types of living creatures, man among them.

Because of widespread literacy, especially among the Buddhist communities in Laos, Thailand, Myanmar and Cambodia, there are handwritten documents everywhere, too many to be kept under one roof of a national archives or a national library. To prevent them from disappearing, field preservation is urgently needed throughout Mainland Southeast Asia. At the time when the region is at peace and regional cooperation is encouraged, especially through the ASEAN mechanism, field preservation can only strengthen regional ties and bring back the memory of a common regional heritage of beliefs, values and wisdom.

This article will outline some of the recent efforts at field preservation in Thailand, Laos and Myanmar. The author has been involved in all of these efforts at different levels.

Field Preservation in Thailand

"Field Preservation" here means in situ preservation and conservation of local written sources using appropriate technology and basic methods of preventive preservation. The documents are not taken away, although important ones would be microfilmed, again in the field. It is in contrast to the library or museum-type of conservation which treats each document with perfect care at great expense. In field preservation and conservation (PAC), there is a race against time. Behind it all is the belief that local heritage should be best looked after by the local people.

Field PAC of traditional manuscripts in Thailand was not practiced on a large scale until the 1960s, when Associate Professor Sommai Premchit started a survey and microfilming project of northern Thai manuscripts from his base at the Social Research Institute of Chiang Mai University with the support of the Toyota Foundation. The project succeeded in cataloguing over 10,000 fascicles or about 3,000 titles and produced 110 reels of microfilms[1]. At about the same time, the Siam Society in Bangkok also supported a survey of manuscripts in northern Thai temples.

A microfilming project was funded by the Deutsche Forschungsgemeinschaft (DFG) in the early 1970s and run by a German scholar, Harald Hundius, and Singkha Wannasai, a local expert in the northern script and literature. The project produced about 1,000 titles in microfilms[2].

Mr Hundius was instrumental in convincing the Government of the Federal Republic of Germany in 1986 to support what turned out to be the largest field preservation effort ever attempted in Thailand. The Project for the Preservation of Northern Thai Manuscripts was run by the newly created Center for the Promotion of Arts and Culture of Chiang Mai University headed by the present author. The Project had three main aims:

- to restore and preserve the traditional manuscripts in about six northern Thai temples;
- to promote awareness of the value of the manuscripts and encourage active participation among the local people in PAC efforts; and
- to establish a model for PAC activities by setting up institutions and network among scholars, monks and lay supporters.

The project emphasized preventive methods, that is to say, safe-keeping of the documents to prevent damage by external factors such as the weather, insects, animals and man. As there was neither time nor budget to carry out extensive conservation measures at each temple, basic "spring" cleaning-up method was used. The manuscripts were dusted and placed in new cotton bags. Palm-leaf manuscripts without wooden covers were provided with new ones. New containers would also be provided wherever possible as the traditional boxes tended to encourage stacking that could damage the manuscripts, and worst of all, place them out of human attention. In some cases they were removed from the original repositories to more suitable buildings. All manuscripts at each monastery were catalogued under a new system which divide them into 21 categories. Each document was given code numbers according to the province, monastery, category, bundle number and title. Important ones were microfilmed. A list of all the documents were given to the each monastery.

Local participation was an important aspect of this project. Monks, novices and lay supporters of both sexes at each location were briefed on the importance of the written heritage and asked to participate in the cleaning, cataloguing and microfilming activities. Over 1,000 local monks and laymen from eight provinces attended workshops that focused on basic PAC methods, the contents of the manuscripts and appropriate organizations for future PAC activities. The Project had hopes to set up "Manuscript Preservation Centers" (MPCs) in each province to sustain PAC activities at the local level. This aspect of the project has not been successful for lack of financial support and the nature of local Thai government, which is excessively centralized.

Nevertheless, as a result of this project, nearly 100 monasteries in upper northern Thailand had their manuscripts catalogued for the first time. Most of them are religious texts, with Jataka tales forming the bulk of the documents. Over 45,000 titles are now on record kept in a database at Chiang Mai University; over 3,000 of them have been microfilmed and available in 325 reels. While there are now many local individuals in the "preserved" areas who know the importance of their heritage and the rudimentary principles and methods of PAC, the documents are still underused and the sustainability of local efforts is in question.

Field Preservation in Laos

Lao manuscript writing belongs to the same tradition as that of the Thais in Thailand. Changes in governmental policies in the late 1980s made it possible to look back for cultural identity in the past. In 1989, a Project for the

Compilation of an Inventory of Palm Leaf Manuscripts was set up by the Ministry of Information and Culture under the leadership of Dara Kanlaya and funded by the Toyota Foundation. Associate Professor Sommai Premchit of Chiang Mai University acted as a consultant to this project which emphasized making inventories of temple manuscripts in seven provinces. However, as the Northern Thai project drew to a close, the German government was asked to provide a similar assistance to Laos. Again, with the help of Mr Hundius, a Preservation of Lao Manuscripts Programme was established with the aim of preserving manuscripts in Buddhist monasteries and other libraries throughout Lao PDR from 1992-2002.

While this project is similar to the Northern Thai project, it is more ambitious as it covers the whole of Laos and would like to make a better use of the manuscripts not only for religious but also for scholarly and educational purposes. It plans to set up a bibliographic database of Lao literature and create a text pool which can also be used for the upcoming revision of the "Lao Literature" curriculum at high schools and other institutes of higher learning.

By the end of 1994, the two projects had covered 222 monasteries in seven provinces and have recorded over 36,000 titles[3].

Field Preservation in Myanmar

Traditional written records in Myanmar consist of palm-leaf manuscripts and folded paper books (parabaik). While many of these records are now kept out of harm's ways in public organizations such as the National Library and the Universities' Central Library, many more manuscripts are in monastic and private holdings throughout the country. They are unclassified and do not receive attention as manuscripts but as holy objects that are worshipped rather than read.

U Tun Aung Chain, Chairman of the recently established National Commission for the Preservation of Traditional Manuscripts, has pointed out that although there was a general consciousness of the need to address the question of the preservation and conservation of Myanmar traditional manuscripts on a national basis, the first concrete steps in that direction were taken only in 1994. One of the precipitating factors was the Conference on the Library and Archives Preservation Needs of Southeast Asia organized by Chiang Mai University Library with the cooperation of Cornell University Library [in Chiang Mai in 1993][4].

The formation of the National Commission in September 1994 under the Ministry of Education was the first of its kind in Southeast Asia. It is composed of members from 12 organizations that are the major governmental custodians of traditional manuscripts, such as the Myanmar Historical Commission, the Language Commission, the National Archives, the Department of Archaeology, the Religious Affairs Department, the National Library, the Universities' Central Library, and the Universities Historical Research Centre.

As part of its work, the Commission has conducted two field inventories. One was at Bagaya Monastery in Mandalay in February 1995. This temple has over 2,000 manuscripts, the labor of its past abbots. The Commission made a listing of some of the vast holdings with active local support. Nearly 900 palm-leaf manuscripts and 232 parabaiks were listed, with the rest reserved for future work. Another was at Nan - Oo Monastery in Paungde, Bago Division in August 1995. Again, the collection in this monastery was the work of the abbot who had a strong interest in traditional manuscripts. Nearly 400 palm-leaf manuscripts have been listed[5]. The Commission has also started on a project to compile an electronic Union Catalogue of Traditional Manuscripts in both public and private holdings. It plans to microfilm selected traditional manuscripts in the future.

Conclusion

Field preservation in Southeast Asia, however small and localized, is always worthwhile, not only because it will reveal the local cultural landscape and memory, but a bigger regional picture can also emerge. Most Buddhist monasteries keep manuscripts related to the Buddhist doctrine, meditation techniques, ethics, astrology and divination, mythology, rites and rituals, medicine, history, laws and customs, poetry and grammar. A regional survey would show connections, similarities and common ground. For example, the history of the Shwedagon pagoda in Yangon can be found in many temples in northern Thailand. The inventory of manuscripts at Bagaya in Mandalay has revealed for the first time the existence of another Myanmar version of Chiang Mai chronicles. Comparative studies in traditional medicine, laws and myths will no doubt give us a better view of the regional knowledge of the past. Such knowledge could plan an important role in reinforcing the present efforts to construct a new Southeast Asian world for the 21st century.

Works Cited

1. Social Research Institute. *A Catalogue of Lan Na Manuscripts Microfilm Copies in the Social Research Institute.* Chiang Mai: Social Research Institute, 1982.
2. Hundius, Herald. "The Colophons of Thirty Pali Manuscripts from Northern Thailand". Reprint from *Journal of the Pali Text Society*,1990.
3. Lao PDR Ministry of Information and Culture. Statistics of Monasteries and Palm-leaf Manuscripts Already Surveyed (1988-94) (in Lao). Unpublished paper.
4. Tun Aung Chain, U. National Commission For the Preservation of Traditional Manuscripts. Paper presented at the Preservation and Conservation Meeting, Universities Historical Research Centre, Yangon, Myanmar, 20-21 November 1995.
5. Ibid.

Rujaya Abhakorn
Department of History
Chiang Mai University
Thailand

[Mr Abhakorn's paper was presented at the 62 IFLA General Conference, Beijing, China, 25-31 August 1996.]

John F. Dean

Collections Care in Southeast Asia: Conservation and the Need for the Creation of Micro-Environments

Introduction

The nations of the upper regions of Southeast Asia have great difficulty in ensuring the survival of their cultural property for reasons that are historic, economic, and climatic. Among the most vulnerable nations are Burma, Cambodia, Laos, and Vietnam. Of all cultural property, library and archive materials are the most vulnerable to damage and neglect, and it is especially tragic as national identity and, indeed, economic recovery, are often seen to be linked to the survival of documentary materials, as libraries and archives form the heart of the fragile educational systems so necessary to the development of viable and competitive economies.

Since 1987, I have worked in libraries, archives, and art museums in all the nations of the region on behalf of the Cornell University Library's Department of Preservation and Conservation, supported by funding from the government of the Netherlands, the Harvard-Yenching Institute, the Henry Luce Foundation, the Christopher Reynolds Foundation, UNESCO, the Swedish International Development Authority (SIDA), Oxfam, the Open Society Institute, and various other non-governmental agencies. The work has been concentrated on attempts to save rapidly deteriorating collections through needs assessments, staff education and training, developing and conducting conservation projects, and microfilming threatened collections to safeguard their textual content.

Burma, Cambodia, Laos, and Vietnam have all experienced savage war and civil unrest in recent years, and recovery from these disasters is difficult and likely to be exceedingly slow. My work in this region of Southeast Asia began in Cambodia amid the devastation of the national library and national archives following the retreat of the Khmer Rouge, and this experience plus more recent work in Burma over the last four years and continuing work in Vietnam has demonstrated the vulnerability of both research materials and librarians.

Before describing the challenges of preservation work in the region, it might be useful to explain why a university located in the rural heart of central New York State should be at all interested in Southeast Asia and its libraries and archives. Cornell was founded in 1865 through the generosity and political skills of Ezra

Cornell and the scholarly endeavours of its first president, Andrew Dickson White. Both men were determined that the university would provide instruction in every subject, that it would be non-sectarian, and enrollment open to all. Cornell is one of that exclusive group of American universities known as the Ivy: League, and it is indeed a large and prestigious research and teaching institution. The nineteen libraries of the university hold a total of approximately 9 million physical volumes, and more than 75 million manuscripts, making it the tenth largest library in the American Association of Research Libraries.

Cornell's interest in Southeast Asia began in 1918 with a donation of 9,000 books and manuscripts from Professor Charles Wason, and the creation of the Far Eastern Studies programme in the mid-1940s. The determined collecting of John M. Echols, a professor of modern linguistics, and Giok Po Oey, the first curator of the Echols Collection, resulted in the largest collection of Southeast Asian books and manuscripts in the world, and facilitated the development of extensive area studies programmemes at the university, as well as instruction in fourteen Southeast Asian languages.

The Department of Preservation and Conservation was established in 1985, and soon became one of the larger preservation programmes among academic research libraries in the United States, and an early preservation initiative was the large-scale microfilming of rapidly deteriorating Southeast Asian materials from the Echols Collection. Copies of the film were presented to libraries in Southeast Asia to help replace collection losses. Preservation field work in the region grew out of the growing concern of faculty and graduate students and the reports of Helen Jarvis, an Australian scholar and librarian. In 1987, Dr Jarvis reported on conditions at the National Library of Democratic Kampuchea, now Cambodia[1] Her report resulted in a more detailed assessment by a Cornell graduate student, Judith Ledgerwood, which was reported at an international conference in Washington[2]. Soon afterwards, applications by Cornell to private foundations paid off with a small award by the Christopher Reynold Foundation which permitted John Badgley, curator of the Echols Collection, and me, to visit Cambodia, Thailand, and Vietnam, beginning what has become a continuing programme of preservation action in the region. The effects of the strife and political upheavals of the past fifty years in the area, however, make the preservation challenges daunting, with materials disappearing through deterioration, theft, and political expediency almost on a daily basis.

Western scholars have been generally, though somewhat vaguely, aware of these problems for some time, but it is only quite recently that the full breadth and scope of the especially difficult problems facing libraries and archives have become known to a few Western librarians, archivists, and preservation specialists. Over the last decade, international agencies, both public and private, have produced spasmodic reports on conditions, and indeed, several successful projects designed to preserve specific collections in particular places have been conducted. These reports and projects were, not surprisingly, limited in their overall effects, and conditions overall remain little changed with materials still disappearing at an alarming rate. However, limited as these projects have been, they have resulted in the preservation of some vital pieces of scholarly information, and perhaps, more important, these pioneering efforts have created a much greater awareness of the crisis. Virtually every report by foreign observers on libraries and archives resulting from fact-finding missions describes dilapidated facilities, undertrained and under-equipped personnel, minuscule or non-existent funds, and collections that are often bibliographically and physically inaccessible. While a few cultural gems, well known to Western scholars, are better protected and available, the vast majority of library and archive materials are not, and local students and scholars alike struggle painfully but determinedly to try to satisfy their research needs.

Burma (Myanmar)

Library conditions in Burma were described in 1968 by Palle Birkelund, reporting for UNESCO. Birkelund described well-organized libraries, competent personnel, and remarkable recovery from World War II[3]. The premier library in the capital, the Universities' Central Library, had been almost completely destroyed by bombing during the war, along with two of the college libraries, resulting in the loss of research materials and valuable scholarly notes. For example, scholar Gordon Luce lost the fruits of twenty-five years of research when the Japanese looted the collection, and the later monsoons destroyed what remained after Allied bombing[4]. Birkelund commented on the need for better environmental controls, insect fumigation, and trained "book binders and restorers" to begin the conservation of manuscripts and other library materials.

Ten years later, a report to UNESCO on the preservation of manuscripts in Burma, produced by V. Raghavan, described a much more desperate situation, with manuscript collections being rapidly diminished because of humidity, insects, lack of trained personnel, official indifference and neglect[5]. Raghavan recommended a series of actions that would have resulted in substantial improvements and a slowdown in the rate of loss. In particular, he recommended that conservation facilities be established to treat damaged and deteriorated manuscripts, and drafted specific plans for improved environmental conditions. Referring to an unpublished UNESCO survey of Burmese manuscripts in 1956-57, Raghavan urged that a union catalogue of manuscripts be developed to encourage inventory control and to deter theft.

In general, little has been done to implement Raghavan's suggestions, either in preservation or bibliographic control, and there are indications that the situation continues to deteriorate further. Thousands of manuscripts have been stolen from Burmese libraries and temples, and are offered for sale as curios in the tourist antique shops and markets of Thailand. In a June 1994 report, Peter Skilling and H.K. Kuloy described their efforts to rescue a few of these manuscripts by purchase in the markets of Thailand, noting that they had managed to save, "750 palm leaf manuscripts in Pali or mixed Pali-Burmese, 18 bundles of Khun palm leaf manuscripts (each bundle contains from 5 to 15 smaller palm leaf sets), 270 Burmese black paper accordion books (Parabaik), and 12 Shan white paper accordion books"[6]. Skilling and Kuloy are still active in gathering these materials and intend to return the manuscripts to Burma "in better times."

Cornell University's preservation involvement in the libraries of Burma began in 1989 with a three year project to microfilm fragile palm leaf manuscripts at the Universities' Central Library in Rangoon. To date, 5,000 manuscripts have been microfilmed, but another 15,000 manuscripts need to be filmed through future projects. The Henry Luce Foundation and Cornell alumni have funded the work, but continuing support is problematic. A Cornell report of 1988 points out that environmental conditions in the libraries were very bad, and that large portions of the general collections were unprocessed and untreated[7]. Cornell's work of preserving research materials in Burma has been carried out in the face of some political opposition and criticism from those opposed to any interaction with Burma, but as a recent report noted, the "rapid deterioration and loss of these [Burmese] materials should not be allowed to continue because of political isolation, as all humankind will be the poorer for their loss[8]."

More recent work in Burma, reviewed in a report of a survey and training visit I made in March 1995, has revealed a slightly more promising situation despite political difficulties and isolation. The Universities' Central Library has initiated some limited preservation efforts on a regional basis, concentrating initially on the region immediately surrounding Rangoon. Modest space has been allocated in a new building for conservation facilities, and the Cornell-funded microfilming efforts are being carried out in a well appointed space in the library, using equipment donated by an early UNESCO project and a more recent gift through the Australian National Library. In addition, some conservation equipment has been installed through Cornell with the help of the Open Society for Burma Institute. At the Rangoon University's Historical

Research Centre, considerable progress is being made in the care of archival materials and the collecting of monument rubbings, and Soe Soe Sein and U Pe Thein, archivists at the Centre, have each recently completed a six months preservation training programme at Cornell. Although facilities and resources are very scarce at the University of Mandalay, large numbers of palm leaf manuscripts are stored in a sensible fashion. Unfortunately, the extreme, and unrelieved, heat and voracious insects are hastening the destruction of these and other library materials. The Royal Palace at Mandalay also has a number of palm leaf and parabaik manuscripts along with numerous photographs, and all are poorly housed in facilities that lack the means to regulate the high temperatures and relative humidity, or to keep out insects. The environment at the Bagaya Monastery Library at Amapura is much more encouraging, with the 6,000 palm leaf manuscripts and large numbers of parabaik being carefully handled in a space that may soon be air-conditioned through donations from devout overseas Buddhists. Students from the University of Mandalay's Department of History, less affected by the university closures in Rangoon, are involved in cataloguing and collating the manuscripts at Amapura, with copies of the data sent to the Universities' Central Library at Rangoon for eventual entry into a database, a substantial beginning step towards Raghavan's 1979 inventory recommendations[9].

Cambodia

The condition of libraries and archives in Cambodia is probably the worst in this region of Southeast Asia. The reports of Helen Jarvis in 1987 and Judy Ledgerwood in 1988 had described appalling conditions, with the libraries of Phnom Penh little more than shells of their pre-Khmer Rouge days. In a report of a preservation/conservation training visit to Cambodia made in April 1989 with a Cornell team, assembled as a direct result of Ledgerwood's report, I identified a number of modest priorities for immediate preservation action[10]. These priorities have largely been addressed by projects stemming from the reports and from a subsequent training project that I conducted in February 1991. In 1989, the National Library was without a water supply, and had only eccentric and very dangerous electrical systems. Less than twenty percent of the collection survived the Khmer Rouge, who threw out into the streets and burned many of the books and all of the bibliographic records. The Library was used as a pigsty for the duration of the Khmer Rouge regime, and of the original National Library staff of 43, only three survived. My report further notes that large mounds of books and manuscripts were piled in the storage areas, many rescued from the streets and markets. The National Archives was badly damaged by insects, and Soviet attempts to control them with DDT were not successful, and I saw similar conditions at the Royal Palace and the National Museum. At the Tuol Sleng Museum of Genocide, a former high school used by the Khmer Rouge as an interrogation centre, more than 20,000 men, women and children had been tortured to death, and significant numbers of confessions and photographs of victims had survived the Khmer Rouge's attempts to destroy them during their retreat. These materials were in surprisingly good condition, although the real danger to the archives seemed to be from Khmer politicians with an interest in their disappearance.

The situation is now reportedly somewhat changed and significantly improved in Cambodia, and a June 1994 news report indicated that the French Government had provided some aid to the National Library of Cambodia by supplying library and binding equipment[11], and Australian archivists working with the Overseas Service Bureau have been improving access to materials in the National Archives. A report by Elizabeth Watt of the International Branch, the National Library of Australia[12] indicates growing library aid activity even without full "normalization". Volunteer staff members from Cornell University have regularly worked in Cambodian libraries over the past 10 years, and a 1998 report of one Cornell staff member Sari Suprato, indicates improved funding from international agencies is helping shape libraries and turn attention toward preservation.

The first Cornell Library overseas training and conservation project began with training sessions at the National Library to begin the process of stabilizing the palm-leaf manuscript collection. This collection was in very poor condition, with considerable insect damage, extensive soiling, and structural damage. The manuscripts were piled in tottering heaps on the floor of the library, many scattered into loose, unconnected leaves. The staff of the National Library was trained to provide preliminary cleaning of the manuscripts by light dry brushing to remove loose soil and insect parts, and to construct protective enclosures that would protect each individual manuscript, and to box small groups of manuscripts in tight, well-constructed boxes containing an insect repellant[13]. The staff quickly became adept at constructing the boxes, and the appropriate conservation supplies and tools were provided through a variety of funding sources in the United States, including the Christopher Reynolds Foundation and the Henry Luce Foundation. I also provided training to ensure that the general collections of the National Library received some conservation attention, and a book repair operation was established.

It became apparent that the survival of some of these unique materials could best be assured by microfilm, as the traditional method of preservation, copying by hand, was impossible given the small number of monks left alive by the

Khmer Rouge. Although the palm-leaf manuscripts seemed a high priority for the Khmer, Cornell also considered that the filming of the Tuol Sleng archives should be accomplished as a matter of urgency. As noted, the archives consist of "confessions" extracted from some of the victims, and some 6,000 photographs and negatives produced as "mug shots" by the Khmer Rouge. The following year, with additional grant funding assured, Judy Ledgerwood, fluent in the Khmer language, began the work of microfilming first the palm-leaf manuscripts and then the archives of Tuol Sleng. Ledgerwood had received intensive training in microfilm camera set-up and operation prior to the project, but the difficulties she encountered were impossible to prepare for, and essentially typical of work in poor countries. Electrical supply at the National Library in Phnom Penh, as noted, was somewhat dangerous and unreliable, and there was no water supply. Ledgerwood purchased a generator to operate a small air conditioning unit and the microfilm camera at the National Library for the filming of the palm-leaf manuscripts. At Tuol Sleng, the old generator was repaired (which proved to be an unwise investment), and a room set aside for filming and new storage for the filmed documents. The factor that proved to be the most difficult to overcome, however, was the refusal of the government to grant formal written permission to film (although there was an informal, oral agreement with the Minister of Culture), and as a result, there was constant interruption of the work by various governmental officials backed by troops and a consequent defection of Khmer project staff. The work to microfilm the 400,000 pages of the 4,000 confessions, the "Manual of Torture," entry log, and "instructions to guards," took from 1990 to 1993, with four different project directors, beginning with Judy Ledgerwood and ending with Lya Badgley. Work in Tuol Sleng was not only difficult because of mechanical problems and political intrigue, but the oppressive and morbid atmosphere also took its toll. Historian David Chandler observed that people using the archives "confront daunting problems...there is the emotional drain of encountering so much cruelty, so many innocent lives destroyed[14]". Before the archive was microfilmed, access to the confessions was difficult, with little time allowed to scholars to study the materials. Chandler went on to note that, "by the middle of 1991, less than 10% of the dossiers had been read and analyzed by scholars, much of which concern major figures in Democratic Kampuchea. The confessions of 3,500 "lesser" victims remain to be studied, and many of these probably contain important historical detail." The archives is the key source of information for the U.S. State Department's Office of Cambodian Genocide Investigations. The film was exposed in difficult circumstances, but initially the processing and inspection was almost equally difficult, with each reel of exposed film taken in the International Red Cross diplomatic bag to Bangkok where it was flown to Ithaca, processed within 24 hours, inspected and evaluated by preservation staff, and results faxed back to Bangkok for delivery to Phnom Penh to effect corrections to the shooting procedures. The Tuol Sleng archives project, in particular, has been an extremely valuable contribution to scholars throughout the world and, in the best tradition of preservation reformatting, has ensured the preservation of material in danger of destruction while extending access to scholars.

By January 1991, Cornell had obtained grant funding to continue with phase two of the conservation work in Cambodia, and I was able to return to Cambodia as part of a more extensive survey visit to Vietnam and Thailand. The conservation treatment and training projects conducted during this visit were extremely intensive, addressing the stabilization of the Tuol Sleng archives through the construction of document cases, the stabilization of palm-leaf manuscripts at the Royal Palace and the Buddhist University, and the conservation treatment of the palm-leaf manuscripts already microfilmed and stabilized at the National Library. Treatment of the palm-leaf manuscripts involved taking them out of the individual enclosures and group boxes constructed in the 1989 project, which provided the opportunity to evaluate the effectiveness of the housing strategy. To my great satisfaction and relief, there had been no re-infestation of the manuscripts by insects, and no additional structural damage had occurred. From July to December, 1998, a staff member from the National Archives, Y Dari, completed a six months' preservation training programme at Cornell, and no doubt some further improvements will be made to the general situation as a result of her influence.

Many of the reports on libraries and archives by Western and Australian librarians seem to imply that the wretched conditions in Southeast Asian libraries are not immediately apparent to native library and archive staff, and must be identified for them by the visiting foreign expert. Recent conferences and meetings in the region, described later, suggest that the local librarians are not only well aware of the deficiencies of their facilities, but have a good general sense of their overall needs.

Laos

The Nordic Institute of Asian Studies (NIAS) report on Laos and Vietnam, produced by Irene Norlund, Jonas Palm, and Stig Rasmussen in the early part of 1991, was designed to provide the Swedish International Development Authority (SIDA) with information on the overall library and archive situation[15]. The team noted that collections in Laos are "insufficiently stored and...unorganized," that the "preservation situation in Laos is virtually non-existent," and the country is in desperate need of basic education and training, materials and equipment to preserve only a small part of its history. The report makes the interesting observation that the traditional method of "preservation" of palm leaf manuscripts was by constant copying to preserve the contents, and that the concept of physical conservation represents "a new way of thinking." Based on a thorough survey and analysis, the report makes some valuable recommendations, especially in the area of long-term support for Laotian libraries and archives.

The concerns reported by the NIAS team on Laos were repeated a few months later by Donna Reid, for the National Library of Australia[16]. Reid noted that palm leaf manuscripts, because of their cultural and symbolic value, were being given top priority for preservation attention by the Lao, and she expressed concern about the lack of attention paid to printed (paper) materials. Training in library science was given by Reid to Vietnamese librarians during this 1991 visit as part of a follow-up to a similar 1990 programme. A pragmatic collections maintenance programme was recommended to initiate a collection stabilization and needs assessment project.

A report in the *International Preservation News* of June 1994 indicates that progress has been made in Laos to resolve at least some of the problems noted above[17]. With the financial assistance of the French government, substantial renovation has been accomplished at the National Library of Laos, some training in conservation techniques has begun, and another assessment of conservation needs conducted by Jean-Marie Arnoult of the Bibliothèque Nationale de France. The project was relatively modest and short-term, however, and the problems remain massive and seemingly intractable. Cornell's work in Laos has been essentially limited to noting the manifest problems cited above through visits in 1992 and 1993, and working with the Loa government to try to establish cooperative programmes that will have a more long-term effect.

Vietnam

Conditions in Vietnam are similar to those described in Laos: deficient library and archive infrastructure (especially in the north), few resources, rapidly deteriorating collections, and few trained staff, although there has been substantial improvement over the last five years. The National Library in Hanoi now has a competently-run microfilming operation and their new building renovations will further improve the storage environment. The Institute of Sino-Nom Research in Hanoi is equipped with air conditioning, and recently, new metal stack shelves. However, some facilities have no glass or screening on the windows, with collections piled on the floor, or crushed into insect-infested wooden shelves. The NIAS report, cited earlier, pointed to the wholesale evacuation of books and manuscripts from Hanoi during the war with the United States, as a contributing factor to deterioration, as many books were destroyed and others still remain in storage or packed in boxes.

I visited Hanoi and Ho Chi Minh in 1991, and observed conditions in libraries in both cities[18]. As might be expected, some of my findings on the state of preservation at that time confirmed other reports, particularly in regard to infrastructure and environmental conditions. In general, conditions were significantly worse in Hanoi than in Ho Chi Minh, not surprising considering the intensive bombing of the North Vietnamese capital and past American support for libraries in the south. The long-term economic embargo imposed on Vietnam by the United States and sustained by her allies, made improvements to the educational infrastructure difficult. The National Library at the time of the 1991 visit was in dilapidated condition, with debris scattered throughout the stacks and books piled seemingly at random. The Social Science Institute Library at Hanoi was stuffed with books, many unprocessed and piled in huge mounds on the floor. Only the Institute for Sino-Nom Research, the archive of the most celebrated manuscript collection in Vietnam, held the promise of a stable environment, as a new air-conditioned building had been constructed and was almost ready for occupancy. In the south, the General Sciences Library is housed in a comparatively modern American-style building constructed in 1974 and, given the lack of resources, very well managed and maintained. This library once had an active microfilming programme, and I noted that the Kodak MRD-2E camera had not been in operation for years because of a missing part.

In February and March of 1995, I had the opportunity to work again in these libraries as part of a project organized by Judith Henchy, Southeast Asian Section Head, University of Washington Libraries, and accompanied by Robert Motice, University Microforms International. The project, sponsored in part by the American Association of Research Libraries and partially funded by the Luce Foundation, was designed to help establish microfilming and stabilization programmes in a number of institutions at Hue, Hoi An, Hanoi, and Ho Chi Minh. I found at that time, while there has been some small improvement in conditions at the National Library at Hanoi, storage and housing continue to be unsatisfactory, and the only changes at the Hanoi Social Science Institute Library were largely for the worse, with access complicated by enormous cataloguing backlogs and severe lack of space, although the Institute itself has added an American Studies Reading Room with funding from the Christopher Reynolds Foundation. Conditions at the Institute for Sino-Nom Research had actually worsened as the new building, occupied in 1992, has proved to be sadly deficient, and in some respects actually inferior to the old building. The new concrete structure was very poorly constructed to an unfortunate design, the air handling system was inadequate and inconsistent and the old wooden shelves responsible for carrying insects from the old building to the new. In May of this year, I conducted an intensive preservation feasibility study at the Sino-Nom Institute and found significant improvement there following the earlier six months of preservation training of the librarian, Chu Tuyet Lan at Cornell[19]. At the present time, Ms Lan is working to establish a conservation programme with funding from the Toyota Foundation.

The University of Hue library also has poor storage facilities, and the collection is over-crowded and very poorly maintained, with insects and mold everywhere in evidence. At Hoi An, the Service of Vestiges Management, responsible for the preservation of regional culture, provided simple but effective storage, and the many stele and Chinese family records are in quite good condition and responsibly managed. At the General Scientific Library at Ho Chi Minh, conditions continue to be quite good, despite over-crowding and heavy atmospheric pollution. The microfilm camera, film processor, and related equipment, inoperative during my 1991 visit, were restored to working order by Robert Motice, and there seem to be some prospects that the original regional newspaper filming role of the Library will be re-established[20]. Other library and archive collections visited in Ho Chi Minh were not as well housed as those at the General Scientific Library, but quite competently organized within the limits of the meager resources.

Cornell's work in Vietnam has involved mainly education and training, with a number of demonstration projects being conducted in various parts of the country, but the recent award by the Harvard-Yenching Institute will permitted me to work for a three-week period to produce a Five-Year Plan for the Sino-Nom Institute in Hanoi, and the final report is in the process of being implemented.

Education and Technical Training

Every Cornell project has included significant training and education components, principally to further the specific objectives of the conservation or preservation aspects of the project, but also to try to establish basic in-house programmes. This training has always been intensive and conducted within a short time-frame, with long hours and often continuous work for periods of up to ten days without a break. The trainer/mentor has always worked alongside the trainees, and I am invariably impressed at the degree of skill and knowledge developed by technicians in such a short period of time. The training given in the 1989 and 1991 Cambodia projects, the 1995 Burma project, and the January 1997 Thailand project are examples of training under quite severe time constraints. For example, in the 1995 Burma project I conducted five conservation training workshops and assessed three collections in six days, and in the Thailand project, Anne Kenney (Associate Director, Cornell Department of Preservation and Conservation) and I conducted four workshops at Chiang Mai University in seven days on digital imaging, basic conservation, and the conservation of manuscripts (this latter project is unusual in that it was funded by the Thai government rather than by an outside funding agency).

Over the last few years, several training and education programmes have been conducted by a number of different agencies in the region, as well as the offering of internships or overseas training opportunities and I will summarize a few of them here. Perhaps the oldest, continuing programme based in Southeast Asia is that conducted by SPAFA, the SEAMO (Southeast Asian Ministers of Education Organization) Regional Centre for Archaeology and Fine Arts. SPAFA was first conceived in 1971, originating in the Applied Research Centre for Archaeology and Fine Arts (ARCAFA). In 1985, SPAFA was officially named, with member countries, Indonesia, Malaysia, Philippines, Singapore, and Thailand, with Brunei Darussalam becoming the sixth nation in 1988. In addition to programmes which include undersea archaeology, ethnography, indigenous fine art, and performing arts. SPAFA has also promoted programmes in the conservation of library and archive materials. Held in different countries of the southern region of Southeast Asia, the training sessions deal with bookbinding and repair, micrographic operations, restoration of photographic materials, conservation of paper documents and plans, leaf-casting, map mounting, lamination, encapsulation, and conservation management. The conservation portion of the programme is heavily influenced by Western bookbinding and restoration tradition, being conducted by European craftsmen, and does not seem tailored to the special needs of Southeast Asia.

In June 1994, two seminars on preservation management were conducted at Bangkok and Hanoi by Wendy Smith, University of Canberra, Australia, and Ross Harvey of the Monash University at Melbourne, Australia. The seminars followed similar programmes at Bangkok in 1992 and at Kuala Lumpur in 1991, and formed part of the National Library of Australia's efforts as regional centre for the International Federation of Library Associations Core Programme in Preservation and Conservation (IFLA-PAC). The then head of the National Preservation Office, Jan Lyall, had been very supportive of these, and other efforts, to establish preservation programmes in the region, and the seminars are a tangible manifestation of the interest of the National Library of Australia.

Funded by the Australian International Development Assistance Bureau (AIDAB), the seminars were intended to engage the delegates in the development of preservation management policies[21]. The workshops conducted in 1992 were thorough and well-planned, with a mixture of theoretical and practical work, and the round of seminars was designed to complement them[22]. Much of the Australian interest in preservation in the region is the result of the pioneering work of Helen Jarvis, who initiated the development of a bibliographic database of Southeast Asian materials. The training programme for Southeast Asian librarians that emerged from Jarvis's work, and broadened by AIDAB, has resulted in library school training programmes in computers and preservation/conservation at the School of Information, Library and Archives Studies, University of New South Wales[23.].

In the American Association of Research Libraries project in Vietnam in February and March 1995, cited earlier, I conducted conservation training workshops at Hue, Hoi An, Ho Chi Minh, and Hanoi, while Robert Motice provided concentrated training in microfilming operations to help establish the programmes at the National Library, Hoi An, and Ho Chi Minh, and he and Judith Henchy conducted two lengthy workshops on the development of microfilming programmes. Motice also installed camera and processing equipment at the National Library.

Following the survey and preservation training visits to Cambodia, Vietnam, and Thailand in 1991, I became convinced of the region's need for a major sustained preservation education and conservation training programme. The short-term nature of hard-won funding has encouraged past efforts that, while effective in rescuing a few important groups of materials and providing incidental training, do not seem to have had a lasting effect on the establishment of preservation programmes. Indeed, it is likely that some of these scattered projects have created a level of expectation among the region's librarians, archivists, and government officials that is unreasonable and unrealistic. There have been attempts, mainly through occasional overseas internships, to train conservators, but thus far they do not seem to have had any lasting effects, partly because the training orientation seems designed to address mainly Western rare and unique items, partly because the necessary operational infrastructure does not exist in the region, and partly because the training is isolated from other efforts. As many of the reports have noted, the preservation problems involve poor environment, slovenly housekeeping, deteriorating paper, and failure to deal with elementary binding and repair problems. Although rare and unique materials represent an important scholarly and cultural resource, at this point their level of use seems to indicate more the need for stabilization and security than for complex, expensive, and largely unattainable conservation treatment. At the managerial level, the training and education provided by workshops, such as those conducted by Wendy Smith and Ross Harvey, and more recently by Jonathan Rhys Lewis (Senior Conservator at the Greater London Record Office) at the Vietnamese National Archives[24], are extremely valuable and an essential ingredient to continued development in the region, but these need to be reinforced by sustained and integrated efforts if lasting programmes are to be established. Lacking operational models and the resources needed to create them, local librarians and archivists find it extremely difficult to compete for attention in bureaucracies struggling with more fundamental problems. Under these circumstances, occasional training sessions seem disembodied and their tenets often hopelessly utopian. It is clear that a great need exists for a more general, broader and pragmatic approach, both in treatment and reformatting with the required corresponding levels of training, and to the education of preservation managers and administrators. It seems logical to establish training programmes based on existing operational practice, involving trainees in ongoing model programmes in the region. As no acceptable programmes currently exist, there is a need to establish one that would fulfill the requirements of trainer, educator, specialized service utility, and continuing mentor.

Regional Preservation Center for Southeast Asia

In March 1991, a plan for the establishment of an international cooperative preservation/conservation centre, derived from my 1991 report, was distributed to a number of parties, including Chiang Mai University (Thailand), the Nordic Institute for Asian Studies, and various international funding agencies. The plan describes a full service centre located at a host institution in an economically and politically stable country in the region, to permit personnel from neighbouring countries to pass freely to and fro. The centre would function as a service facility, undertaking the preservation/ conservation work of the host institution and specialized work of other institutions on a cost-recovery basis. Trainees from around the region would serve as interns at the centre, working at a range of tasks in ascending levels of difficulty according to their needs and levels of expertise. Training would operate on two levels, administrative and technical.

Administrative training would expose potential preservation administrators to some of the practical aspects of preservation through short training sessions in the operational units of the centre, but the primary focus would be on programme development and managerial skills, needs assessment techniques, strategy planning, and proposal writing. Interns at this level would be librarians and archivists.

Technical training would be designed to develop skills and increase knowledge. Interns would work in the appropriate operational unit at the centre, acquiring skills through practical apprenticeships. Because of the realities of local programme development and to maintain momentum, interns would be trained on an intermittent basis, and would work at the centre in the area most relevant to his/her needs for three months, then would return to the home institution to implement the newly acquired procedures and in turn, to train local staff. After an appropriate period, the intern would return to the centre for more advanced training.

The centre would be staffed by a skilled and knowledgeable working group, who would assist the establishment of local facilities by site visits, but more important, would act as continuing mentors. In this role, the centre staff would advise and encourage former interns, and supply technical back-up and specialized, capital-intensive services. The interaction of centre staff and interns from the nations of the region, would inevitably forge formal and informal cooperative links that would lead to the development of a solid body of knowledge and professional activity.

In 1991 I made an intensive consciousness-raising trip to Denmark, Sweden, the Netherlands, and Germany, and representatives of the Foreign Ministry of the Netherlands expressed their willingness to provide funding for a conference to be held in Southeast Asia to solicit opinion and grassroots support for the centre. The resultant three-day "Conference on the Library and Archives Preservation Needs of Southeast Asia" was held at Chiang Mai University in December 1993, and was attended by 37 participants from six countries. The national libraries of Thailand, Burma, Vietnam, and Laos were represented, as well as other important institutions. In all, 16 papers were delivered by scholars, librarians, and archivists, detailing the vital importance of traditional texts of each nation, and describing their most pressing preservation needs. In the discussion following the papers, there was general agreement that the libraries and archives in the region faced almost identical problems with only a limited number of solutions, that only concerted action could bring about positive change, and there was unanimous support for the establishment of a centre. Accordingly, a representative development committee was created to develop a planning strategy, and the resultant meeting at Chiang Mai in September 1994 led to the establishment of a consortium with the following mission:

- Establish a system for the exchange and sharing of information on preservation strategy and related activities among members;

- Develop education and training programmes in preservation management and conservation practice;
- Help to facilitate the creation of preservation programmes in each member library and archive; and
- Establish a regional cooperative centre for the preservation and conservation of library and archive materials.

In November 1994, a document was drafted, "The Preservation and Conservation of Library and Archives Materials in Southeast Asia: Outline of Funding Needs," and distributed to various funding agencies in advance of any proposal. As a preliminary response to the needs articulated in the mission statement, and at the specific request of the consortium members, in July 1997, Cornell initiated a preservation and conservation internship programme for Southeast Asian librarians and technicians with the funding assistance of the Henry Luce Foundation, the Harvard-Yenching Institute, the Open Society Burma Project, and various Cornell alumni.

The internship is a three-year project to provide managerial and technical education and training through six-month internships within the Department of Preservation and Conservation at the Cornell University Library. The Department has a staff of 30 involved in a comprehensive programme of preservation and conservation, and there is a great deal of collective experience in addressing the special problems of Southeast Asian materials and libraries, and in training through internship. Over the last ten years, Cornell has trained 25 librarians and technicians from other institutions through formal internship, including nine through an Andrew W. Mellon Foundation programme and 16 through a New York State programme. In addition, there have been several internships supported entirely by Cornell, including two Fulbright Fellows from the United Kingdom and a librarian from Burma. In October 1995, another Fulbright Fellow from Guyana began a six-month programme in preservation, and in September 1996, a librarian from Chiang Mai (Thailand) completed a three-month internship.

Because Cornell's preservation programme is designed to deal realistically with all the preservation problems essentially typical of all libraries and archives, interns are able to develop an understanding of the integrated nature of preservation within the managerial structure of the library, and to apply a range of strategies that stress the setting of priorities and the articulation of needs. Cornell takes two interns at a time, and it is hoped that the programme will stimulate local programmes and help build some of the infrastructure that will hasten the establishment of the Centre. Thus far, interns from the National Library of Thailand, the Sino-Nom Institute of Hanoi, Burupha University in southern Thailand, the House of Representatives Archives in the Philippines, the National Archives of Cambodia, the Historical Research Centre of Burma, the University of Malaya, and the General Sciences Library of Ho Chi Minh city have been involved in the programme. Mentoring visits by Cornell staff to reinforce the training and help further the development of preservation programmes are funded from a variety of sources.

Conservation Strategy

While the Cornell internship programme is designed to expose interns to all aspects of preservation, including complex conservation treatment, digital imaging, microfilming, and various managerial functions, there is no doubt that without resources, training alone will not achieve speedy results. Many of the problems manifest in libraries in Southeast Asia require substantial investment to be fully addressed, but they can be significantly ameliorated by a more systematic approach to environmental control and housing, which can be achieved at modest cost. Wooden shelving can be gradually replaced with metal, windows can be screened to prevent the ingress of insects, a higher standard of cleanliness can be maintained, more responsible handling procedures established, and protective housing can be applied or improved.

It is undeniably very expensive to alter a large environment, such as a large stack space, but a measure of control can be obtained by creating micro-environments. Protective enclosures, such as boxes, portfolios, and map cases, not only add an insulating layer to reduce the effects of varying levels of temperature and humidity, but also can provide other opportunities for control. For example, in a facility with serious insect problems, the large-scale fumigation systems employed by many libraries and archives are harmful to books and readers, and are only temporarily effective. But a well-made box can contain and retain a mild insect repellent that will deter insects, and has the added advantage of being effective even when the material is transported to another location. A steel map cabinet with a base can be treated through placing a dessicant and insect repellent in the base itself to help safeguard the contents of the cabinet from mold and insects. Protective enclosures can be made quite easily from models that are readily available and generally do not require complex and expensive equipment or even extensive skills. While it is extremely risky to entrust a valuable book or manuscript for treatment by an untrained technician, there is little risk in having the same technician construct a protective enclosure.

A systematic survey of library and archive collections will reveal numerous instances where protective enclosures can produce more stable environments as well as protection. The survey can also provide the basic data from which a long-term preservation strategy can be developed, which in turn can help to articulate preservation objectives that can be achieved through sensible funding proposals to international funding agencies.

Conclusion

The body of preservation knowledge and practice on which Western systems are built is the result of a long and torturous evolution from the wholly craft/trade-based bookbinding tradition, to the present level of quite sophisticated and highly technical programmes. The libraries and archives of Southeast Asia have operated to a very different time-frame, and set of cultural and historical circumstances. The industrialization that revolutionized the West in the 19th century was barely known in Southeast Asia until the modern military conflicts of the second half of the 20th century. Solutions to preservation problems are not entirely the same in the East as the West, and the few attempts to inflict Western standards and practice, unaltered by locale, have been unsuccessful. For example, the stock response to high levels of temperature and relative humidity by Westerners is to call for air conditioning systems to be installed. This can be a costly mistake in tropical regions, especially when books and manuscripts are taken from the library, or when untrustworthy electrical supplies fail[25]. In these circumstances, the drastic increase in temperature and relative humidity causes moisture condensation on the materials and interior walls and consequent rapid development of mold. In Southeast Asia, it is important to recognize that preservation priorities are probably not the same as in the West, that short-term teaching and training alone will not result in viable programmes without sustained financial support, preferably secured by librarians in situ, and that the Western response to deteriorating materials and adverse conditions must be learned from experience with the advice and support of the people of the region. Preservation projects should build towards the achievement of some coherent plan, and all projects originating in the West, whether for training or preservation production, should be seen as merely transitional to the time when the nations of Southeast Asia are able to mount and support their own preservation programmes to begin to stem the tide of deterioration sweeping over their collections.

References

1. Jarvis, Helen. "A Visit to Kampuchea 9th to 23rd July 1987: A Report." *Southeast Asian Research Group Newsletter* 35, 43-48.
2. Ledgerwood, Judy. "Worldwide Efforts to Preserve the Khmer Language Materials". (Paper presented to the Second International Conference on Cambodia, Washington DC, 30th September 1988).
3. Birkelund, Palle. "Burma Libraries," UNESCO report, April 1969.
4. Gosling, Andrew. "Burma and Beyond," *National Library of Australia News* VI (No. 13 October 1996) 2.
5. Raghavan, V. Preservation of Palm-Leaf and Parabaik Manuscripts and Plan for Compilation of a Union Catalogue of Manuscripts. Paris: UNESCO, 1979.
6. Skilling, Peter and Kuloy, H.K. "Fragile Palm-Leaves: Manuscripts Preservation Project." January - June 1994.
7. Badgley, John. "Research Report: Higher Education Libraries in Burma." February 1988.
8. Badgley, John. "Exchange and Conservation Programmes," Burma Debate 2 (No. 2, April/May 1995) 30.
9. Dean, John F. "Preservation and Conservation in Burma: A Survey and Training Project at the Universities' Central Library and the University of Mandalay, 20th to the 28th of March 1995. Report to the Open Society for Burma and the United States Information Service".
10. Dean, John F. "Preservation Survey and Conservation Visit to Thailand, Vietnam, and Cambodia, 7th January to 8th February 1991."
11. "Cambodia," *International Preservation News* 8 (June 1994).
12. Watt, Elizabeth. "Report on a Visit to Cambodia and Vietnam, 9-16 May 1993." International Branch, National Library of Australia.
13. See Dean, "Preservation of Books..." American Archivist for detailed description of the forms of enclosure and methods of construction.
14. Chandler, David P. "Brother Number One: A Political Biography of Pol Pot." Chiang Mai, Thailand: Silkworm Books, 1993.
15. Norlund, Irene. Jonas Palm and Stig Rasmussen, "Libraries in Laos and Vietnam: A Report from a Consultant Mission on the Library Sector.16.2.1991-9.3.1991." Copenhagen: Nordic Institute on Asian Studies.
16. Reid, Donna. "Report on Second Consultancy to the National Library of Laos and Other Vientiane Libraries." July 1991.
17. "Laos." *International Preservation News* 8 (June 1994).
18. Dean, John F. Preservation and Conservation in Burma: A Survey and Training Project at the Universities Central Library and the University of Mandalay, 20th to the 28th of March 1995. Report to the Open Society for Burma and the United States Information Service.

19. Dean, John F. The Library Collection of the Sino-Nom Institute, Hanoi: A Feasibility study on the Establishment of a Preservation Programme. May 1999.
20. Dean, John F. "Conservation in Vietnam: A Project to Support the Microfilming of Deteriorated and Non-Deteriorated Library and Archive Materials, February 22nd to March 19th, 1995. Report to the Henry Luce Foundation".
21. Smith, Wendy. "Preservation Management Training in Southeast Asia: AUA APSIG Library Preservation Seminars 1994," *Cite* (December 1994).
22. Harvey, Ross. "Report: ALIA-APSIG Preservation Management Workshop, Bangkok, April 1992".
23. Giese, Diana. "Focusing on Southeast Asia." *National Library of Australia News* 10 (July 1996).
24. "People," *Library Conservation News* [British] Preservation Office No. 51.(Summer 1996).
25. Lee, Mary Wood, *Preservation Treatment of Mold in Library Collections with an Emphasis on Tropical Climates: A RAMP Study.* Paris: UNESCO, 1988.

John F. Dean
Cornell University
Ithaca, New York, USA

[Mr Dean's paper was presented at the 65th IFLA Council and General Conference, Bangkok, Thailand, 20-28 August 1999 and published in *International Preservation News* 20 (December 1999).]

Helen Shenton

Macro and Microenvironments at the British Library

Macroenvironment

British Library Building at St Pancras

The new building for the British Library became fully functioning in the summer of 1999, when the last of the collections moved to the St Pancras site. The final stage comprised 200,000 monographs, 25,000 serial titles and 30 million patents of the Science Reference and Information Service (SRIS). Previously the Oriental and India Office Collections (OIOC), the Humanities, Philatelic, Music, Maps and Manuscripts collections moved from various locations around London into the new building over a two-year period. There has been a phased opening of the 11 reading rooms.

The controversial building designed by Sir Colin St John Wilson has opened to great acclaim, particularly for the light airy feel of the entrance hall and other public areas and for the use of natural materials such as brick, leather and travertine marble.

The building lies between Euston, St Pancras and Kings Cross railway stations and is in an area of North London due for regeneration. It is situated on a very busy, dirty six-lane main road. The building is approached across a wide piazza, under which are sited the main collection storage areas comprising four layers of basement.

The basements house 12 million volumes (approximately 6 million volumes remain off-site) in a variety of different types of storage depending on the different physical media and levels of security. The majority of printed books are shelved on mobile shelving (240 km out of 340 km of all the shelving is mobile) made of galvanized, polyester powder-coated, mild steel. Other physical formats, such as microfilm, sound recordings, maps, seals, scrolls, papyri, works of art and photographs have specific storage furniture, again made of inert material.

Whilst the majority of the collection at St Pancras is stored in the basements, material is also stored in the glass-fronted King's Tower housing King George III's library, and in other high security areas above ground including the exhibition galleries. In addition, reference material is on open access in the reading rooms. The amount on open access varies depending on the type of collection, for example, nearly 50% of SRIS material is on open access compared to 5% in Humanities. The collections are brought up from the basements and elsewhere to the reader by means of a Mechanical Book Handling System (MBHS) and the items are located and tracked by an Automated Book Request System (ABRS).

Throughout the building there is a fire alarm and detection system (FADS) with 4000 smoke detectors. The sprinkler system is a "wet" pipe system. Inergen is used as a fire suppressant in the strong rooms and plant room. There is closed-circuit television and alarmed doors throughout the building. For emergency preparedness, in the basements there are freezers and vacuum packing machines, as well as salvage trolleys and salvage materials throughout the building.

Environmental Parameters

One of the main reasons for building a new library was to improve the storage conditions of the collections. The majority had previously been housed in the British Museum which did not have air conditioning.

Particulate filtration levels are specified at 5 micron in the new building and atmospheric pollutant levels are monitored. A computer-controlled system maintains different lighting régimes within the building. Natural lighting is used extensively in the reading rooms augmented by artificial light. UV is excluded whenever possible. The specification for light levels in the reading rooms is 350 lux; in the storage areas is 50 lux. In the exhibition galleries fiber optic lighting of <50 lux or <200 lux is maintained, depending on the light sensitivity of the artefact on display. The galleries opened in April 1998 and the light levels are being monitored in the galleries as part of the rotation of objects. The environmental specifications are as follows.

	Relative Humidity	Temperature
Collection storage areas (basements and strong rooms)	50% ± 5%	17°C ± 1°C
Public areas, including Reading Rooms	50% ± 5%	21°C ± 1°C
Exhibition Galleries	50% ± 5%	19°C ± 1°C
Photographic store	45% ± 2.5%	15°C ± 1°C

Early Assessment of Achieveability of Specifications

The Conservation Department has instigated weekly environmental monitoring using dataloggers to verify the BEMS system and check non-monitored areas. There are inevitable teething problems with the environmental control of the building for a number of reasons, ranging from non-exhaustive testing before occupation, to local plant being too powerful, to naturally evolving changes in use of parts of the building as its 1200 occupants moved in.

A conservator is responsible for monitoring the environment on all the BL sites. A weekly report is compiled, detailing which areas are within specification or if not, if they are within specified outer bounds, or if they are outside even the outer bounds. The outer bounds are a pragmatic approach to the environment in that whilst the highest standards are aspired to, it is recognized that in a new building this is not necessarily achievable immediately at all times and therefore the amount by which the environment is outside its specification carries different degrees of risk. Currently, the environment is within the specification for 60% of the time, within the outer band for 39% and outside that for 1% of the time.

In the exhibition galleries the cases, made by Glasbau-Hahn, have individual air conditioning separate from the general environment in the exhibition area. There are 5-10 air changes an hour. The original specification was 17°C ± 1°C, 50% ± RH 5% inside the cases and 21°C ± 1°C, 55% ± 5% in the gallery for the comfort of the visitors. For a variety of reasons this proved very difficult to achieve, not least because when the books, manuscripts, and other artefacts were put into the empty cases the bulk of the organic material had a buffering effect, it is thought, leading to greater fluctuations in temperature and humidity. A compromise of 19°C ± 1°C, 50% RH ± 5% RH is now in place both inside and outside the cases. There have not been any complaints from the public about the lower temperature. The cases are monitored by the BEMS system and double-checked with dataloggers. If the environment goes outside the outer bound, which is specified as < 40% or > 60% RH, < 16°C or > 22°C the public vacate the areas while the problem is solved. The lighting in the exhibition area is being logged, using Lux bugs (Hanwell Instruments) to calculate the cumulative light exposure of artefacts to help decide when to rotate them.

The new building has undoubtedly led to great improvements in the macroenvironment in which the British Library's collections are held. The need to measure the impact of that environmental improvement on the rate of deterioration will be a future challenge. For the BL's library and archival collections, the methodology using isoperms, or adaptation of the "time weighted preservation index" used for photographs are possibilities.

Microenvironment

Enclosures - Boxes

The British Library uses a variety of different types of microenvironments whether boxes, enclosures, folders or envelopes made from a variety of materials. For boxes it mainly uses drop-back boxes made of archival millboard covered with archival buckram (acrylic coated) and lined with archival paper; "phase" boxes made of archival manilla tied with a button and tie, and a conservation adaptation of the wraparound, folded case (based on *chit-su* and *tao* boxes), made of archival mountboard, covered with a cotton cloth, lined with archival paper and held with bone toggles. Flap-case folders and envelopes (both of archival manilla and inert polyester) are used; slip cases are not used.

There are many different considerations which dictate which type of enclosure is chosen, some economic, some practical, some aesthetic. The comparative costs of the three main types of box are shown in Table 1.

Table 1: Comparison of boxing costs

Box type	Price
Drop-back box	£50.00
Chit-su-type box	£50.00
"Phase" box - see table 2	£4.50-£12.77

The different types of boxes give different degrees of protection to the items inside and will endure different amounts of handling. The drop-back box is the most robust. The "phase" box, developed by Christopher Clarkson at the Bodleian Library at Oxford, is so-called because it is regarded as the first phase of a book's conservation treatment. In reality it is often the only treatment a book will receive. Phase boxes can be bought as ready-scored flat packs which can be made up by anyone, not necessarily a conservator. However they are not available in an infinite number of sizes and so the box may need to be packed out to accommodate the volume snugly. Phase boxes can be made by hand, using a hand- or hydraulic creaser to fit an individual item and take about 35 minutes to make. There are now computer-operated machines which make phase boxes and take about 6 minutes. For example, the National Library of Scotland and the British Library have a Kasemake Box and envelope-making machine (CXD KM503). The comparative costs for the different sorts of phase boxes are shown in Table 2. These machines can potentially be programmed for cutting mounts and it may be possible to develop them for making cradles for book display.

Table 2: Comparison of phase box costs

Phase box	Price
Inhouse - hand made	£11.45
Inhouse - boxing-making machine	£4.50
External	£12.77

A third type of box used at the British Library is a conservation adaptation of the wraparound, folded case, of the Japanese *chit-su* and Chinese *tao* boxes. This is used almost exclusively for stab-sewn, limp paper, often multi-volumed oriental bindings.

Boxing projects

At the British Library improvements to the microenvironment of individual items is often done on a project basis. In particular there were many boxing projects before the moves into the new building, not only to minimize risk of damage during transit, but to improve storage and handling once on the new site. For example, all the palm-leaf manuscripts which are particularly vulnerable were boxed prior to being moved.

Since moving to the new building the opportunity has been taken to examine work practices, organization and treatment. So, for example, the six furbishers have become the Collection Care Section, dealing with a wide range of preventive conservation and maintenance including cleaning, immediate repairs and box making. They have just changed from making boxes by hand to operating the Kasemake machine. Given the scale of the conservation need at the British Library the work is carried out on a project basis. For example, a large collection of 10,000 unbound European manuscripts in the Oriental Collection are particularly vulnerable when being transported from the storage area to the reading rooms and their treatment was conceived as a project. Examination of the treatment options, ranging from microfilming to fasciculing to encapsulation to binding to boxing, determined that the latter was the best option both from curatorial and storage points of view.

Interaction of Macro- and Micro Environment

It is very simplistic to divide storage neatly into macroenvironment and microenvironment as the two are obviously interconnected. Sometimes the one will be used to combat problems with the other. In the new British Library building, the environmental specification of photographs in the Oriental Photographic Store was proving difficult to achieve (15°C ±1°C, 45% ± 2.5%RH,). Therefore as an interim measure dataloggers were placed inside the store, inside an empty box, and inside a drop-back box which already had photographs in it and the results were compared. The environment within the boxes was stable, compared to the cycling pattern outside. As an interim solution therefore, the photographs will be boxed to create microenvironments until the macroenvironment of the store is solved.

Future Developments

Macroenvironment and microenvironments are only part of the care of the collection. At the British Library all the elements which affect the storage are being formulated into "Levels of Collection Care". This is adapted from the UK's Museums and Galleries Commission "Levels of Collection Care" which define basic, good and best practice in terms of handling, etc. In that the British Library still has a number of stores both within London and in the North of England which are not to the highest standards of the new building, the aim is to ensure that everything is at least at a basic level of care.

In the area of microenvironment the British Library is looking into the use of an anoxic (oxygen-free) environment for storage of some parts of the collection. Work at the University of Cambridge suggests this is also useful for magnetic tape. Vacuum-packing of newspapers has already been used in libraries (such as the State Library of New South Wales) but anoxic storage would involve introducing oxygen scavengers and oxygen-level indicators. This is being investigated as part of a large project to preserve the newspaper collection, and might be used for storing newspapers in poor condition which have been microfilmed. The use of newly developed materials such as Microchamber paper and board, which absorb pollutant offgassing, is also being looked into as part of this project, as well as the use of acid scavengers. In addition, vacuum packing is being investigated as a technique for accelerated drying of water-damaged items in the event of a flood.

Helen Shenton
Deputy Director, Preservation Collection Management
British Library,
London , UK

[Ms Shenton's paper was presented at the 65th IFLA Council and General Conference, Bangkok, Thailand, 20-28 August 1999.]

Toshiko Kenjo

Preservation Environment in Library Stacks and Anti-Disaster Measures

The Climate in Asia

The climate in Asia varies according to three zones: temperate, tropical and desert. Japan, Korea and China are located in the temperate zone where the average precipitation is 250-550 mm in winter, and 1,000 mm in summer (500 mm in China). Moreover, Korea and Japan are humid in summer because of the very humid seasonal south wind and have low levels of temperature and humidity in winter because of a low northern wind. India and Vietnam suffer from a tropical climate: 2,000 mm in summer and 250-550 mm in winter. Temperatures rise up to 30°C. In Vietnam floods and storms occur regularly in summer. Mongolia lies in the desert zone and receives very little rain (below 50 mm throughout the year). A continental sand-laden wind blows continuously and the average temperature is 15°C.

This range of variations entails different preservation methods. While in Korea and Vietnam, cultural properties are mainly made of paper-based works of art, excellent for moisture absorption and desorption, in Mongolia, documents are inscribed on stones and jewels. Keeping such characteristics in mind, it is important to take the most appropriate measures to preserve each type of cultural property in the future, thanks to global communication.

The Environment in Underground Stacks

It is well known that wall paintings or tomb furnishings kept in tombs have been preserved in good state. From this we assumed that the environment in ancient tombs was ideal for preservation. According to a five-year survey on annual temperature differences, which I conducted at the Torazuka old tomb[1] in Ibaraki Prefecture (north-east of Tokyo), the temperature difference was very small throughout the year: while the average highest temperature was 30°C and the lowest temperature was 5°C in the open air, in the tomb, the average highest temperature was 17°C and the lowest 15°C. Relative humidity was always around 100% in the tomb. This showed that temperature and humidity changed little in the tomb, while they changed dramatically in the open air. However, the fact that relative humidity in the tomb was stabilized at 100% showed how humid the soil in Japan was. In fact, underground stacks have always suffered from humidity and mold.

So before the underground stacks of the National Diet Library were built, much research and discussion were conducted. A special waterproof system was developed. First, a concrete wall was built over the soil. It was sprayed with a mortar gun and smoothed with trowels. Then it was covered with primer. A waterproof asphalt sheet made of non-woven fabric for civil engineering use was used for lining. Rubberized asphalt was sprayed over the sheeting. This completely blocked out humidity from the soil. Over this base, concrete was cast and the building frame was made. Inside the building frame, specially manufactured boards containing thermal insulating and moisture prevention materials were attached. Stacks for rare and old materials are made of wood, which absorbs and desorbs moisture.

Stacks have eight floors underground and four floors above. The first floor of the building is waterproofed efficiently to prevent water released from the fire extinguishing system from pouring down to the ground floor. As stacks are located deep in the ground, soil shuts out air from the outside.

The temperature is kept at 22°C± 2°C, and humidity at 55°C ± 5%. If no one enters the stacks, the temperature difference during daytime is 0.7°C, and the humidity difference is 0.8%. The stacks for rare and old materials are equipped with a separate air-conditioning system in order to blow fresh air into the stacks, which saves energy. The atrium was installed to allow sunlight to flow down to the eighth floor below. It also helps reduce changes of temperature and humidity within the stacks, as the thick air layer shut off from the open air by the windows on the second floor acts as an effective heat insulating layer.

Fire Prevention

The underground stacks of the National Diet Library are equipped with smoke detectors, which, in case of fire, inform the central control room automatically, the Disaster Prevention Centre of the NDL, and then the fire station. Stacks are also equipped with emergency broadcasting equipment to give evacuation orders to staff. Halon gas is used for fire extinction. Stacks are arranged so as to avoid the accidental exposure of staff to gas. They are divided into two areas. In case of emergency, central iron doors shut down automatically. Elevators work on an emergency electricity supply. Within the glass window of the atrium, an automatic smoke protection shutter has been installed. There are three entrances/exits between the closed stacks and the atrium. The second underground floor and those below have earthquake-resistant walls. Floors are resistant not only to earthquakes but also to external earth pressure. The heads of the stacks are locked into place by square piping in order to prevent them from falling over.

Above-ground Stacks: Traditional Wooden Construction

Contact with the open air makes it very difficult to preserve materials in the stacks above ground. The greatest cause of deterioration of old Japanese documents and books is the phenomenon of "mure". "Mure" is a climatic condition that arises from a combination of high temperature, high humidity and lack of air circulation. Old documents and books in Japan suffer from heavy deterioration between June and the end of September, namely from the rainy season to the typhoon season.

Our predecessors invented unique and excellent construction methods such as gable roofs, traditional soil walls and raised-floors, to prevent "mure" and dew condensation. In Kyoto and Nara, constructions are made of wood. Gable roofs keep off sunlight. "Ranma", an openwork transom above the sliding partitions beween two rooms, prevents "mure", because warmed air moves through the openings. Long eaves give shade to the walls and protect them from the rain. In order to avoid dampness, the floor is raised. Under the floor ample space is created to prevent "mure" and decay.

Gable Roofs Protect the Surface of Walls

Also characteristic of Japanese constructions is the soil wall, traditionally called "shin-kabe", which means "heart wall" or "central wall". This wall absorbs and expels air moisture. Wooden pillars and lintels are at ground level and hold soil walls. Wood and soil are materials which absorb and desorb moisture while kraft paper, diatomaceous earth[2] and China clay hardly absorb and expel moisture. If walls had been made of such materials in Japan, dew condensation would have been caused.

Our predecessors must have invented construction methods using wood and soil to live comfortably, although indoor humidity reaches 60% to 65% even when it rains and when outdoor relative humidity rises to 100%. Thus it is important for preservation, to keep the indoor humidity level as low as possible. Gable roofs can be compared to hats. Eaves protect the surface of walls. The basics of preservation are to take care of the heart of the house. Based on these ideas, modern construction methods have invented new materials such as heat insulators.

Description of the Imperial[3] Household Agency

The building of the Imperial Household Agency has one story below ground and four stories above ground where precious documents of the Archives and Mausolea Department[4] are stored. It stands on a small hill with an adequate drainage system. No air conditioning is needed but only natural ventilation. Roofs are gable-shaped, thermal insulating materials have been used for the ceiling in the attic, walls have been made up of heat insulators and air layers, and porcelain tiles have been used for the external wall. Interior walls are made of Japanese cedar which tempers humidity. The building has windows on its eastern and western walls, and balconies on its northern extremities to allow the air to flow readily through the storage rooms. In case of disasters, the eaves and disaster protection shutters of balconies and windows work automatically.

This building is excellent for maintaining temperature. The annual minimum temperature on each floor is 6.5-7.0°C, when it is -1.7°C outside. The differences of temperature and humidity between daily maximum and minimum on every floor are very small, less than one tenth of those in the open air.

Gable roofs are shallow and do not have large attics. The fourth floor temperature is 28°C, while it is 23°C on the first, second and third floors. This is because the attic does not have a sufficient air layer. However, the bulk of documents will increase so rapidly over the next few years that attics are considered to be a waste of space. In modern constructions, thermal insulating materials are used, and have the same function as attics. But if thermal insulating materials are used, they are useless as they have no layers. Instead thermal insulating materials should be installed in the ceilings.

Ventilation openings should be installed in gable roofs in order to avoid the "mure" phenomenon. As mentioned before, "mure" occurs when artefacts are stored in hot and humid environments that are not ventilated. A gentle flow of air helps prevent "mure", as a gentle wind is valuable for the preservation of old documents and books. However, when the temperature is low, no wind is necessary. The effectiveness of the thermal insulating materials attached to the fourth floor ceiling of the storehouse of the Imperial Household Agency were studied. The temperature and humidity were surveyed by a thermo-hygrometer in the ceiling, under the heat insulating materials, and on the fourth floor.

The survey was conducted from July to October when "mure" occurs frequently. The temperature under the heat insulating materials was low, while the temperature in the attic was very high. The gable roof was an excellent invention by our predecessors, but the idea of thermal insulating materials using scientific technology is also commendable and makes it possible to use the fourth floor effectively. The ideal prevention measure against "mure" is fresh air ventilation with temperature and humidity a few degrees lower than in storage areas. Windows should not be opened from February to May when the outside temperature is much lower. In the rainy season when temperatures are over 25°C, ventilation should not be operated and air conditioning should be used instead, or a large ceiling fan should be turned slowly in the storage area.

Measures against Particulates and Exhaust Gases

Ventilation is necessary in the "mure" season from June to September. But when windows are opened, sunlight also gets in together with dust filled with exhaust gas. A window panel was invented to eliminate particulates. The panel has a compound structure: nylon filters are attached to both outer sides of the panel to eliminate particulates containing exhaust gas. Inside the nylon filters are micro-filters which eliminate bacteria and mold spores. The innermost part consists of honey-comb papers (5-10 cm thick), which reduce air velocity and control humidity. The panel, named the "window panel" is mounted in the window. After a month, nylon filters are almost black and inside filters are dark too, which shows that contaminants cannot be completely eliminated. Nylon filters were examined through an electron microscope and certain kinds of tars were observed. It is thus probable that exhaust gas had entered the storage area in the form of ultrafine particulates. Ideally the panel should absorb all contaminants, which is not the present case. Its design needs to be improved in the future.

Ideal Preservation Box

Under harsh climatic conditions such as in Japan, old documents and books are stored in boxes. In order to avoid moisture, traditional boxes have legs. For instance, at the Shosoin Treasure House in Nara, double boxes are used to store this precious material. Old documents are covered with "washi", traditional Japanese paper or cloth wrappings, and stored in boxes. The materials the boxes are made of vary according to countries in Asia: in Japan, "paulownia" (a Japanese tree), Japanese cedar and Japanese cypress are used to prevent "mure", because they can absorb and expel moisture humidity. On the other hand, in China, where humidity is lower than in Japan, solid wood such as rosewood and ebony is used. Were preservation boxes to be kept within other boxes made of thermal insulating materials, changes in temperature inside the boxes would become minimal. The same phenomenon happens in ancient tombs where artefacts are preserved from the open air. In other Asian countries, the use of preservation boxes is recommended.

Effects of Preservation Boxes

Changes in temperature and relative humidity inside the preservation boxes were measured. After accustoming empty boxes to the stacks environment for a while, open air was introduced into stacks for one hour. The air temperature changed by 2.5°C while the temperature within the boxes changed by 0.6°C. The humidity level in the open air changed by 13% while that inside preservation boxes changed only by 1.2%. Results show that temperature and humidity hardly change within preservation boxes. If double preservation boxes were used, changes would be even less.

Contamination of Resin[5]

In the past, wooden materials for preservation boxes were dried naturally and sufficiently until no resin was emitted. Nowadays, because wooden materials are dried artificially, the resin remains. When such materials containing resin are used for boxes or stack walls, resin is emitted. You may have the same experience in your house. As long as rooms in modern houses are tightly shut, resin cannot be emitted into the open air and remains within the room. The monomer ingredient of resin is attached to pillars. But when you smell a woody fragance, it means that resin is in the air. Today both stacks and houses are airtight, which results in resin damaging walls.

If preservation boxes are stored before the wood smell appears, resin becomes attached to the surface of the boxes and forms brown spots, not to be confused with resin. On the contrary, resin becomes the nutrient of mold whenever humidity rises. Mold is likely to grow where resin lies. Even though preservation boxes are thought to be effective, new wooden boxes themselves emit resin which sticks to the documents. As resin is acid, paper will turn brittle, just as is the case with acid paper. This is the reason why environment monitoring strips should be used.

Environment Monitoring Strips

As litmus paper tests the quality of water, environment monitoring strips are used to test the air. When the air is almost normal a slight green color appears, which turns yellow when there is acidity in the air, and blue when there is alkalinity. Strips also change color when solvents are in the atmosphere. Books should not be preserved in stacks or boxes before a normal atmosphere is confirmed.

Cleaning Liquid

Particulates enter stacks or preservation boxes. Adhering particulates cause mold or deteriorate paper. Eliminating dust is a basic requirement for preserving cultural properties. However when cleaning is done with water, the humidity level increases. Documents should be stored in boxes after these are dried up. We use a cleaning liquid mainly made of polyvalent alcohol, such as propylene glycol. This cleaning liquid is still under development.

In the experiments done with paulownia boxes, relative humidity within boxes was 62%. It rose to 84% when boxes were wiped with cloths containing water but when the cleaning liquid was used, relative humidity only rose to 65%. This liquid cannot sterilize bacteria but does eliminate them. If boxes are tightly closed, bacteria can be eliminated for about 10 years. Even if temperatures rise to around 40°C, mold does not grow. This liquid cleaning should be very effective in the post-treatment of books from floods in Vietnam and in eliminating the effects of sandstorms in Mongolia. It also protects musty materials from mold. The liquid has to be sprayed and covered with a sheet but it is even better if documents are wiped before being stored. However this liquid can dissolve oil paint, so caution should be exercised.

Methods against Disasters

Wooden boxes burn easily, so we conceived boxes that could have the same function as storehouses to protect materials against fire. However boxes made of general non-combustible materials cannot be closed tightly, so we created boxes made of calcium silicate, which has characteristics in common with wood. These boxes can be given various shapes and can absorb and expel moisture. They can be shut tightly and are strong enough to withstand being crushed by forces from above.

A fire-proof experiment was carried out by putting the boxes in a furnace. The temperature was raised to 1,000°C within eight minutes and then left at this temperature for about 30 minutes. The temperature within the boxes rose to about 130°C. Usually paper changes color slightly at 140°C and turns brown at 180°C and, although we did not notice anything, some changes in the paper occurred at 130°C. The preservation boxes are not able to resist fire completely but are considered one of the best means of preserving cultural properties against fire. The ideal box will be one which can keep an inside temperature of

40°C and relative humidity from 60% to 65%, even if left at 1,000°C for one hour. If such boxes existed, staff could find cultural properties safe even after returning from evacuation. In the future, advanced thermal insulating materials which have been developed in space shuttle research, will be used to create ideal preservation boxes.

From now on, not only papers but also films, magnetic tapes, disks and images will be the most important carriers in libraries. We have to prepare facilities which will have the proper function of preserving them. So far in Japan we have not elaborated standards for the preservation of new media and we would like to cooperate. Last but not least, as a result of the cooperation between staff members of the NDL, architects and staff of the Archives and Mausolea Department and architects, excellent storage places have been created. The important thing is the opinion of staff members. I hope that preservation staff and architects will work hand in hand to cooperate and develop new preservation methods.

References

1. The Torazuka old tomb is supposed to have been constructed in the middle of the 7th century. It is famous for various wall paintings and many kinds of iron work such as swords and arrowheads.
2. "Diatomaceous earth" is a porous rock made of fossilized frustules used in filters, insulators, abrasives, etc.
3. The Imperial Household Agency is in the Imperial Palace in the centre of Tokyo. The Agency is under the control of the Prime Minister and is in charge of the affairs of the State as far as the Imperial House and the Emperor's acts are concerned. It has the custody of the Imperial Seal and the Seal of the State.

4. The Archives and Mausolea Department is in charge of the preparation of the entry of the Imperial Genealogical Book and its custody, the care taking of the Imperial Mausolea and Tombs, the care taking of books and records, the compilation and custody of official documents and all that regards "Shosoin" (the Imperial Repository).
5. "Resin" is an adhesive non-flammable polymer, usually insoluble in water but soluble in organic solvents, such as alcohol.

Toshiko Kenjo
Researcher Emeritus
National Institute for Cultural Property
Tokyo, Japan

[This paper was presented in November 1996 at the symposium organized by the PAC Regional Centre in Tokyo to celebrate its 10th anniversary. Dr Kenjo's article was originally published in *International Preservation News* 15 (August 1997).]

Lin Zuzao

The Traditional and Modern Preservation of Library Rare Books and Precious Materials in China

Everyone knows that China is one of the world's oldest civilizations and has a recorded history of more than 5,000 years. The history of book collecting in China can be traced back for 3,000 years. Literature, in the form of books and precious materials, were handed down from dynasty to dynasty. The current estimate is that there are more than 2.2 million volumes surviving which were published before 1794; 26.45 million volumes of books before 1911; more than 29,000 titles of journals and magazines, and over 7,800 newspaper titles which were published before 1949. Moreover, there are great numbers of manuscripts, rubbings from stone inscriptions, Confucians canons, etc.

In the Zhejang Library, which is located about 200 km to the south of Shanghai, there is a large collection of older materials. It contains inscriptions on bones or tortoise shells of the Shang Dynasty (16th-11th century BC); more than 20,000 pieces of rubbings from stone inscriptions; 130,000 pieces of original printing block plates, a wonder of the library world; stone tablets dating from 1245 AD; Chinese paintings more then 200 years old; more than 180,000 volumes of rare books, some of them dating from the Sung Dynasty; 1.2 million volumes printed before 1911; a total of 3.9 million volumes, comprised of books, journals, newspapers and other library materials.

One may wonder how the ancient Chinese librarian preserved all these library materials. Actually, there is a lot of knowledge to know, to understand, to study. What I am introducing is only one drop of water in the great ocean.

Create a Proprietary Environment Condition for Library Materials Preservation

Ancient Library Buildings

In order to provide a safe environment for the rare books, the ancient Chinese librarian studied and analyzed the relationships between the raw materials of the book, water and fire. Water can fight against fire. Fire can destroy any kind of organic materials including paper, bamboo strips, silk or cotton, etc. Therefore, we have to take special care of these three elements.

Not only can water control fire, it can also help plants grow. Because of this characteristic, the ancient Chinese librarian placed the library in a botanical garden. The botanical garden can create a place of quiet and restfulness, a pure and fresh surrounding for reading. A good example is the Tianyi Ge, which was built in 1566. It still exists. In front of the library building, there is a water pond, which leads to the Great Dongning Lake. The building is surrounded by different kinds of trees and flowers. For enriching the environmental condition, the owner of the library added a pavilion and artificial rocks. All these created a very typical garden setting for the library building, as well as for the safety of the rare books. The owner of this private ancient library had his own residence built side by side with the library building, but separated by two parallel walls. In this way, the calamity of fire could be prevented from entering into the library building. Moreover, there was a specific and strict rule that fire and candle could never, be allowed to enter into the library building.

To Kill or Drive Away the White Ants, Bookworms and Other Insects

It is well known that white ants, bookworms and spiders are the greatest enemies of paper and books. A high degree of moisture creates a suitable condition for these insects to flourish. Therefore, the ancient Chinese librarian had found and used a lot of methods for killing and preventing these insects from invade the library.

Caustic lime or lime-sulphur was spread around the corners of the stack room. If it was difficult to obtain caustic lime, charcoal could be used instead, because charcoal absorbs moisture in the stack room. White arsenic can keep away or kill white ants. If trees or flowers were grown round the library building or a water pond or canal was built near the building, they could create damp, which is suitable for the reproduction of the white ants. Therefore, it was necessary to dig the ground beam of the outside wall of the building for 30-50 cm, spread white arsenic and backfill after that. This kept the white ants away for at least more than 30 years.

Special Care of Rare Book Preservation and Conservation

For keeping away the bookworm (or silverworm) and other insects from the books and preserving rare books in good condition, the ancient Chinese librarian developed a number of methods to preserve them.

In order to keep rare books in good shape, NANMUM wooden plates were used at the bottom and on the top of the book of the whole set which was then tied up with cotton thread. This kind of wooden plate never changed its shape and always remained in a dry condition. Another advantage of this treatment was that it kept the rare book away from dust and free from damage, as well as made it easier for the librarian to use and serve his readers.

Camphor wood was employed to make the holding boxes camphor wood box has its own aromatic smell, which can drive away the bookworm or other kinds of insect.

The smell of camphor ball (or mothball) is one of the most important materials to keep away the bookworm or other insects from the rare books. This kind of camphor ball volatilizes slowly. So, we have to change it after a certain period of time, normally, once a year.

Air circulation in the stack room as well as in the book-holding boxes is also very important. Therefore, when we put rare books in a camphor wood box, we should never pile them up and/or store them close together. Otherwise, when the natural temperature and moisture changes, storage conditions deteriorate.

If a rare book needs to be repaired, the following steps should be observed: 1) Take the book apart slowly and carefully; 2) Straighten out every page of the paper; 3) Starch or size with a special paste; 4) Take a proper weight to press and flatten it in time; and 5) Use silk or cotton thread to bind it again.

Book Drying

Normally, there is a rainy season, which occurs in May and June of the year in the area of the middle and lower Yangtze River. So, we have take special attention to avoid the rare books becoming moldy. In my library, there is a tradition of drying the books in the shade in the open air. We still use wooden boards of (normally China fir) 200 cm x 40 cm for this special work. If a book becomes wet and we do not treat it in time and becomes soggy, it is best not to treat it in a hurry but to find an experienced expert to treat it properly. The expert will put it into a food steamer (usually made of bamboo) to steam it in order to make it soft, and then separate the pages one by one page, slowly and carefully, and then dry it in the open air in a shady place.

Medical Herbs

Famous Chinese medical herbs are used not only for curing sickness, but also for preventing it. The Chinese librarian made a clever move by using some of the herbs to preserve books. Some of the following methods were used and got a good result; 1) Putting the dry leaves of the herbs into the book directly, to let the smell of the herb drive away the bookworm and other insects. The herbs included tobacco leaves, lotus leaves, the herb of grace, etc.; 2) Putting the herbs together with paper raw materials to produce insect repellent paper, for example: Huang paper (with sulphur), Jiao paper (with pepper), Wangnien Hong paper (with arsenic); and 3) Making a special paste and pasting it on the paper, and letting it dry, and then putting this pasted paper in the books.

Using Modern Science and Technology to Preserve Rare Books and Precious Materials

In this new century with the development of modern science and technology, we have adapted and created modern techniques and equipment for the preservation and conservation of rare books and precious library materials.

Scanning

Scanning the library literature and storing it on laser disks is not a new technique. Actually, scanning was developed at the beginning of 1960s and by the end of 1970s, the digital laser disk appeared. Since 1980, this technique was employed for the storage of library materials. At this time, the Chinese Central Government has not developed a general plan to for this method of preservation, but our National Library, the Shanghai Library and my own library (Zhejiang Library) are employing this technology. I believe that starting and completing this work will not only be a major benefit for the preservation of the library rare books and precious materials, but will facilitate the sharing of library resources.

Freezing

The Chinese librarian had studied the living conditions of the bookworm (silverworm) and found that it would freeze to death at a temperature of 40°C below zero. Therefore, some of the libraries in China use this method to kill the bookworm. Our National Library, Shanghai Library and some university libraries have used it. Some archives in China also used this method to preserve other paper-based materials in archives. The disadvantage of this method is that the container of the freezer is too small, for the bookworm should be frozen to death after 48 hours at 40°C below zero, so we have to spend a lot of time and manpower to do this work.

Microwave

The Chinese librarian has found that the bookworm can be heated to death in the microwave oven. A special microwave oven was designed, produced, and used in some of the libraries in China. But this procedure raised two problems. After heating in the microwave oven the rare books become warm and there was concern that the heat may harm the books. Use of this method for killing the bookworm (or silverworm) is very slow. As a result it is not employed in many libraries.

Vacuum Packed

After studying this method of food packing, the Chinese librarian used this technique to pack rare books in libraries. We put those books which are seldom used or have already been microfilmed or have been scanned onto laser disks into a plastic bag, and seal it, and then put these plastic bags with books into camphor wood boxes in order to preserve the books safely. Nanjing Library had used this method and obtained very good results. The advantage of this method is that it does not cost too much. On the other hand, if a book needs to be consulted, it has to be taken out the plastic bag and the seal is broken.

Constant Temperature and Moisture

Modern climate control equipment for air circulation, employing the air conditioner and the dehumidifier, create a condition of constant temperature and humidity. Climate control systems create a very suitable environment in the stack room for storing the library's rare books and precious materials. The Chinese librarian fully understands the advantages of this new equipment. Therefore, in the provincial level libraries, especially when new library buildings and designed and constructed, almost all of them are equipped with these systems. Such is the case in the Beijing Library (National Library), Shanghai Library, Nanjing Library, and Zhejiang Library.

Summary and Suggestions

Protection against natural disasters is a common concern, not least for librarians. Over the centuries librarians have accumulated a great deal of experience and have developed excellent methods for the preservation of rare books and library materials. Libraries constitute a precious heritage and the methods employed in conservation and preservation need to be well publicized. Therefore, I would like to make the following suggestions.

We need to be in constant communication on the subject of preservation of library materials, exchanging our experiences and techniques, especially between Western and Asian libraries.

We must publicize successful experiences in preservation and conservation of the library materials.

We should form a special research group for the preservation and conservation of rare book and precious materials.

Zuzao Lin,
Research Librarian,
Zhejiang Library,
Hangzhou, China

[Dr Lin's article was first published in *International Preservation News* 19 (July 1999).]

Alain Roger and Christophe Hubert

Digitization Aids the Preservation of Globes

Since 1973, Alain Roger, who began his career as a restorer of large format documents in the Bibliothèque Nationale de France, has been putting his imagination and talent to work dealing with globes damaged by time and use. Globes in a parlous state, often perforated, are sent to him by all French institutions. Thanks to the painstaking work of his team, he is able to restore them in spectacular fashion.

The first globes were used in Arab and Chinese civilization. In the 10th century, the Arabs made celestial and terrestrial globes. In Europe, the oldest manuscript globe is attributed to Martin Behaim and dates from 1492.

The production of globes increased in the Renaissance, with the renewal of science and the great discoveries. The globes were made up of gores engraved on wood or copper then printed on laid paper, cut out and glued onto cardboard spheres covered with paste. They were usually produced in pairs, with a celestial globe accompanying a terrestrial globe.

In the 16th century, the technique of smooth cut engraving flourished in Flanders and in the southern part of the Low Countries, which was an important scientific centre. Dutch globes spread throughout Europe due to the skill of the engravers and cartographers and the maritime power of Holland.

French globes dominated in the 18th century, because of their precision and elegance, but British globes were also in demand as, thanks to the voyages of Captain Cook, they filled in the last gaps in knowledge of the world's coastlines.

In the 19th century, production became industrialized, parallelling the spread of education. In our time, geopolitics has imposed a frantic pace of production, coupled now with mass marketing of globes of all types, notably interactive or hologram globes, but of varying quality.

Since the beginning of the 20th century, early globes have been subjected to deplorable conditions of preservation. Sharp changes in temperature and humidity have provoked the cracking of varnish and dilation of plaster and cardboard; while the accumulation of dust has made paper dirty and map detail illegible. Light has also been a cause of damage. However it is also the particular shape of the globes which has led to recurring damage such as that caused by blows which make holes in the cardboard structure, scratches caused by the rubbing of an off-centre sphere against the brass horizon table or meridian, or wearing away of the engraving due to finger pressure on a particular place. The join of the two cardboard hemispheres, glued around the equator, remains the weakest part and has suffered the greatest damage.

Principles of Restoration

Despite developments in the use of materials, the method of production has remained remarkably stable for centuries: a sphere is composed of two hemispheres of cardboard which are joined between the poles by a wooden central axis. They are covered with plaster on which are glued gravure-printed gores. The latter are re-glued, then varnished. The globe is given balance by small bags of lead affixed at the join between the hemispheres on the inside of the shell.

Every restoration is preceded by bibliographic research. Throughout the process, a photographic record is built up, and this dossier accompanies the globe after it has been restored. Analysis of the component elements is needed to identify the materials and the causes of damage, and to discover the technique of manufacture. It also allows identification of previous restoration efforts. Esthetic and historical analysis of the globe begins with a. visual examination. Several scientific techniques are employed to supplement this data: the varnish can be micro-analyzed in natural and UV light; micro-chemical analysis identifies pigments, ink and binding agents, and the chromography of the various layers. Endoscopy is used to directly observe and evaluate the internal elements. The endoscope is introduced into the globe by the hole made near the central axis. Thanks to the technique of scanning, damaged areas are identified and recorded.

Once the globe has been dismantled, the parts made of wood and metal such as the base stand and the horizon table are entrusted to a restorer specializing in cabinet-making. The parts must be placed on a work surface corresponding to the size of the globe. A crate filled with dried sand or glass balls may be used, or else a suitable metal support may be built.

Several techniques must be applied to restore the various components of the globe. It can be cleaned using a dust exhauster or a jet of compressed air and a soft brush.

Traditionally the varnish is removed from the gores with a cotton pad soaked in a solvent made up of one third white spirit, one third ethanol, and one third methyl-ethyl-acetate of acetone. This work is done under an extractor hood, by circular movements, until the varnish is removed, while avoiding prolonged contact between the cotton pad and the surfaces bearing water-colors.

Surface cleaning by ultrasound consists in breaking the layer of dust and varnish down into fine particles, without in any way affecting the surface. The ejected particles are picked up by an exhausting system. The low power rating of the device avoids any heat damage.

It commonly happens that fragments of gores are found glued onto the original gore. This is because until the end of the 17th century, the outlines of the continents, including Europe, were still vague and longitudes imaginary. As it was too expensive to make a new globe, corrections on small pieces of paper were added to existing globes.

Materials Deriving from Medical Research

Removal of the gores and the two polar caps is a very delicate operation because the colors are transient. One may have recourse to steam, or else wrap the globe in GoreTex "Lamine". Once removed, each gore is immediately cleaned of particles of plaster and glue. It is glued on a stretched backing of hemp or japan paper. Experience shows that for perfect restoration it is preferable to fill in missing areas directly on the sphere a few days after refitting the gores.

Then one can proceed to restore the plaster and the cardboard globe. The globe is cleaned of crumbled plaster, and splits are enlarged and cleaned. Cracks are restored by means of a brush dipped in synthetic glue. The plaster used is of the same type as the original, generally with a base of rabbit-skin glue, whiting and kaolin. Dental plaster may also be used.

For the restoration of the cardboard sphere, Alain Roger was inspired by the materials used for orthopedic protheses: 2mm-thick ORFIT "S" prosthetic plates. When held under water at 55°C and first cut to the required dimensions, the plate becomes transparent and malleable for a few minutes. It is then placed on the undamaged part of the globe to which it moulds itself while becoming opaque again. Introduced into the globe at the precise place where cardboard is missing, this prothesis is kept in place by simple pressure and acts as a support for restoration. The cardboard is then restored with tiny spots of paper or cardboard pulp pasted with methylcellulose. The fragile area around the equator, as well as the areas where a lot of plaster is missing, are restored with plaster tape.

Reassembling and Refitting the Gores

To make good areas where gores are missing, a Vinector or Geset leafcasting table is used. However the mixture of fibers used does not allow reproduction of wire marks or chain lines. This technique is adequate for filling in small surface defects and scratches in the paper.

It is very difficult to reconcile ethics and esthetics in paper restoration. For Emmanuel Kant, ethics may be subject to judgment by law and esthetics primarily gives pleasure to the senses, sensation, and cannot be legislated for. Reassembly of missing parts of gores has been done for 15 years and is now universally accepted by French and German restorers and those in the English-speaking countries. As globes are decorative objects, this procedure allies esthetics with scientific accuracy.

Large gaps are therefore made good by laser photocopies of original gores. If these cannot be traced, a new engraving is made from the copper plates. Globes were produced in series, and sometimes the original gores or plates can be found. If not, the gaps are filled in by hand with ordinary restoration paper.

An intermediate paper should be pasted between the sphere and the gores. After the equator and the location of the gores have been calculated and traced, paste is put on half the sphere and on the gores which have been previously moistened. All the gores are fitted and pressed with a bone blade through moistened conservation tissue in order to avoid wrinkles. This operation is repeated 72 hours later for the other hemisphere.

Once all the gores have been refitted, they are pasted again to make the paper more impermeable, to make the colors more stable and to prevent the varnish from impregnating the paper. Then a first coat of varnish is applied, followed by some retouching to correct the colors, then a second coat of varnish. In the case of some rare and prestigious globes, a protective perspex cover is made. Its two transparent shells cover the globe and protect it from dust and from clumsy fingers.

A Revolutionary Method: Digitization of Gores

It was a meeting with two digital imaging specialists, Christophe Hubert and Laurent Lucot, that gave Alain Roger the idea of using software for creating spherical images to reproduce the gores flat, starting from a globe in good condition. The principle is based on mapping work carried out by observation satellite. Photogrammetry[1] consists in "reproducing a globe in a plane representation, from which all types of projection may be drawn, including gores." These methods are technical refinements arising from a patent of the Atelier Holographique, Paris. Photography is a means of non-destructive rapid analysis: approximately two days are required to set up the session and take the photos.

It is essential to proceed in three stages: first, the globe is photographed digitally, "from pole to pole, according to the direction of the gores" using a very high quality color camera giving a resolution of 1000 x 1500 pixels in 24-bit colors. A resolution of 300dpi and perfectly rendered colours are obtained on a globe 50cm in diameter.

There is no loss of quality when loading the images into the computer. Each shot is positioned on a virtual globe according to the angle at which the photo was taken and then the projection of the spherical image is calculated. The smallest characters may be digitized 10 pixels high and still be quite legible.

Nevertheless the overall lighting of the image must be reworked, as there are differences in luminosity between the top and bottom of the globe which produce a scale effect foreign to the original object. Thirdly, the calculated projections are reproduced on paper, by output of final film.

The restorer's role is at the second stage, during image processing. From then on it is up to the restorer to eliminate a brown spot due to foxing or to replace a missing letter by searching for the same letter elsewhere in the word.

Digitization Offers Numerous Advantages

Digitization of a three-dimensional object, a globe, can help in restoration when the gore of the globe to be restored has too many gaps, or it is too damaged, or original prints no longer exist. There are no longer any of the difficulties involved in restoring and refitting gores. There are no more problems with dilation of paper or with delicate replacing on the convex form. However a prerequisite for digitisation is that a copy of the globe to be restored must exist and must itself be in good condition.
The different stages of cartography of a globe may be revealed (for example, correction slips which have been stuck on top of each other).

Digitization allows on-screen restoration of damaged parts, as is done already with paintings and ancient monuments. This method resolves the conflict inherent in conservation, namely between preservation and access. For this reason, it would be desirable in due course for digitized images of gores to be archived and made available in reading rooms or for remote consultation.

Electronic consultation may be by photographic gores (from the North Pole to the South Pole) or by particular projections (unfolded cylindrical, conical or gnomic[2], which makes it possible to compare globes and maps, by virtual aerial survey of the globe. The reader's eye then acts like an aircraft or observation satellite.

The researcher can use various functions for analysis, such as a short or long zoom on the documents, the merging of several topographical layers (for comparison of a globe with another representation of the earth's surface), and access to place names in a thematic database. This technique also makes it possible to transform the projection of a plane map into another projection, and create a globe from a map of the world.

On the other hand, consultation via the Internet is more difficult because of to the basic transmission principle: the "tele-reader" requires the visualization of a portion of the spherical image which the Web server must calculate in order to transmit it to him. However it is almost impossible - that is, it would take far too long - to download the spherical image of a globe at the transmission speeds currently available for general public use.

The researcher may also study a globe in the form of printed gores, and in dimensions larger than the original if he desires. This allows greater reading comfort owing to the size of the gores and the fact that they are being read flat. The large paper widths currently available are quite adequate and affordable.

The restored globe is held back from consultation, and may then be kept in suitable conditions for preservation.

Finally, the decorative aspect of early globes can be appreciated afresh. Thanks to restoration using the most recent techniques, we have available to us a work which is esthetic, legible and ready for consultation, just as it was when it was created.

Notes

1   Photogrammetry is a technique for associating one color with one point in space, based on a photograph. Aerial photogrammetry is a technique for making "photographic" maps from aerial photographics of the ground.

2   A type of projection frequently used throughout the history of
cartography.

References

Roger, Alain and Monique Pelletier. "La renaissance des globes de Coronelli (1650-1718) au Musée des Beaux-Arts de Lille" in *La revue du Louvre et des Musées de France*, 4, 1993.

Hubert, Christophe and Laurent Lucot. *Photogrammétrie sur globes*. Paris: Atelier holographique, 1998.

Alain Roger,
Chef de Travaux d'Art
Bibliothèque Nationale de France

Christophe Hubert
Specialist in Digital Imaging
Ets Oculaire
Paris, France

[The article was originally published in French in *International Preservation News* 17 (May 1998). The English translation was prepared by Winston Roberts, former Coordinator of Professional Activities at IFLA.]

The Photographic Archives of the City Hall in Lisbon

The Institution

The "Arquivo Fotografico da Camara Municipal de Lisboa" (AFCML) is the photography collection of the city of Lisbon, Portugal. It was created in 1942 to assemble the many photographs scattered throughout several departments of the City Hall. The acquisition of several new collections of photographs in the 1940s and 1950s, some of them important to the study of the history of Lisbon and of Portuguese photography, attracted the attention of the public to this institution. It was opened to the public in the late 1970s.

It was only in 1990 that the city hall decided to renovate the "Arquivo Fotografico". The long tradition of use by the public was an important factor in this decision. The AFCML was given new facilities in a building devoted to this very institution. It includes a storage room with insolation and environmental control, an exhibitions room, dark rooms and a reading room. It was the wish of those responsible to achieve the best conditions possible for the preservation of photography collections to make access to images as easy and as fast as possible, and to start a programme of exhibitions and catalogue production to publicize the photography collections. The new facility was opened in 1994.

The Collection

The images are mostly scenes of the city of Lisbon. They show several aspects of the city, such as architecture, urbanization, social and political events, and cityscapes. Portuguese culture is another featured subject. Recently the "Arquivo" has also acquired artist prints.

AFCML holds about 350,000 images, dated from the 1970s to today. The main periods represented are 1900-1920 and 1940-1950. The collection is made mostly of black and white negatives, on glass and on film, and black and white prints. There are many fewer color images than black and white.

The collection grew significantly during the renovation and after the new facilities were opened in 1994. Since 1990 about 100,000 new images have been added to the existing collection, including private donations and purchases. This enormous growth is a challenge to our capacity for treating, cataloguing and digitizing a great number of new images, considering the limited resources and staff (seven conservation technicians and six cataloguing and digitizing technicians). In order to address the needs of the increasing number of images, the conservation treatment of new collections was simplified. We want to reduce the time a collection must undergo treatment before it is made available to the public.

Use of the Collection

The collection is intensively used, both by the public and by the various City Hall departments. The number of visitors averages 2,000 per year. One thousand of them are first time visitors. The number of print requests is about 600 photographic prints and transparencies a year, and 8,000 computer prints a year. We can assert that public interest as mirrored by the number of requests is beyond all the expectations we could have had before the renovation.

Readers are mostly students, teachers, photographers, journalists, retired people, architects and art historians. Seventy percent of our student visitors are studying at the college level. Images are mainly viewed on computer screens. Copy prints are available in the reading room from the images that have not yet been digitized. The reading room provides 14 computer terminals for the use of readers using our database (LISI.).

Computer images are stored on the computer hard disk in PCX format. The computer catalogue format includes the following fields: caption, image local and date, author, collection, bibliography, exhibitions, and copyright restrictions. Image and Boolean research are possible through the computer. The part of the collection available through the computer is the most searched and used.

Conservation Strategies

The main focus of the conservation procedure is preservation. The collection storage room is kept at 18°C (75°F) (+/- 1°C) and 40%-45% relative humidity. The excellent insolation of the walls and ceiling allows the archive to maintain these conditions throughout the year, quite independently from the exterior weather. Great attention is paid to the regular servicing of the air-conditioning equipment. Photograph enclosures were also chosen according to the most demanding preservation requirements. Metal enameled cabinets, neutral cardboard conservation boxes and binders and acid-free conservation paper (Portuguese made), were selected to store the negatives and prints in the main storage room. The above conditions are the guaranty of the stability of most photographic artifacts.

Another aspect of our conservation activity is our concern to reduce the handling of our originals as much as possible. The viewing of photographs on the computer screen is a key aspect of this protection. The use of computer-generated prints for research instead of photographic prints is another important element. The use of cotton gloves to handle prints and negatives is the golden rule at AFCML, followed by all the technicians including dark room printers.

A negative duplication programme was established in 1996 in order to replace unstable nitrate-base negatives and also some acetate and glass negatives in bad shape or deteriorated. These were duplicated onto polyester base, a very stable, modern negative base. The duplication work is carried out in our darkrooms.

The activity of photography restoration is reduced to the most basic aspects. It is viewed as a process of stabilization in cases of broken glass negatives, emulsion lifting stabilization, and torn print stabilization. We do not go further than basic treatment and we take no risks in this field.

Working Procedures

We have settled two rules that are followed as much as possible:
- Compatibility should exist between the project and the resources available; and
- Every conservation project should be followed by a presentation project such as an exhibition or catalogue. These two aspects of our work should always go hand in hand.

In order to make the treatment of new collections more sound and more consistent we have created a standard for procedures. According to this standard, the first step is observation and pre-inventory of the new collection. We do this in order to know the extent of the collection, to identify the processes needed, the present physical shape and the main problems, if any. We also need to ascertain what the necessary housing materials will be, if duplication is required or not, the number of technicians in charge and the prediction of time and costs. Steps for treatment are then defined and a calendar is drawn up for the conservation treatment. Then a decision is taken on the making of a catalogue or of an exhibition of this collection. Treatment generally consists of general description, cleaning, arrangement, numbering, housing, digitizing, cataloguing and duplication (or copy) procedures. Afterwards the collection is made available to the public. Sometimes it is exhibited and a catalogue is published.

The images that we digitize are the result of selection. Low quality images and images that are very faded or heavily deteriorated are rejected, as well as those images that do not fit in our organization purposes. However, these are described in another database that is available for consultation. Avoiding identical images in the computer is also necessary and a survey is done so that only one, in a group of similar images, is digitized. This selection allows us to significantly speed up the treatment of the collections.

The help of interns has been very useful in activities like inventorying the archives, cleaning negatives, organizing, digitizing, and cataloguing. This work is mainly significant in the treatment of the small collections lately acquired. We have interns from Portuguese schools and from institutions that own photography collections. Some come from Spain and Brazil.

We hold many negatives that have no prints. Digitized negative images are converted to positives by computer software so that we can show and supply these images to readers. This also saves photographic paper and a lot of darkroom work.

Accomplishments

After six years of hard work we have digitized and computer-catalogued about 60,000 images (20% of our collection). We have held six major exhibitions of our collection (including catalogues), and several exhibitions of individual photographers. The "Arquivo" has an important role in the conservation of photography in Portugal and is often asked for advice and help. In December 1997, we organized the "Encontros de Conservação de Fotografia", with participants from Portugal, Spain, France, Mexico, Argentina and Brazil.

Luis Pavão,
Photography Curator,
City Hall of Lisbon
Lisbon, Portugal

[Mr Pavão's article was originally published in *International Preservation News* 17 (May 1998).]

Marie-Lise Tsagouria

An On-site Automated Binding Workshop at the Bibliothèque nationale de France: Political, Economic and Technical Considerations

For many decades, a true love-hate relationship has been existing between the Bibliothèque nationale de France (BnF) and private binders. To understand this situation, you have to remember that, in our country, there are more than 700 companies involved in library binding. For most of them only one or two people are working, the craftsman and - sometimes - his wife. The turnover is also proportional: from 20,000 to 40,000 euros. So, faced with this dispersed private sector, the BnF appears as the uncontested leader of the customers.

Since 1990 when the project of a new building for the national library first began, an ambitious programme for the systematic binding of new books entering the library has been devised, which scared the private sector faced with this enormous demand.

The aim of this programme was to reduce the future costs of maintenance or replacement of books as much as possible. But for the binders - and for the library - that meant a complete change of scale: around 10,000 books bound every year in the old library instead of 175,000 in the new programme. For such a difference of scale, a new policy was to be worked out and the necessary resources had to be adjusted to get the desired result, that is an increase in technical quality and a fall in costs and lead times. So, the purpose of this article is to explain how and why it was decided to implement in the new building an on-site automated binding workshop.

Once the decision had been taken to bind all newly acquired materials or those or coming from legal deposit, the resources able to carry out this programme were identified. That gave birth to the very first question: was the private sector able to respond to the new needs of the BnF, both in terms of quality and of quantity?

In 1993-1994, the library commissioned the Tetra Company to carry out a study covering two topics: first, the description of the economic situation of binding firms and then, an assessment of four possible scenarios to implement the binding programme.

The conclusions of the study were the following: the private sector had almost no financial capacity of investment, no will to regroup, and a certain form of opposition to any technical change. This lack of industrial culture was certainly not compatible with the new needs of the library.

Then, four scenarios were assessed:
- completely off-site binding;
- completely on-site binding, managed by library staff;
- completely on-site binding, managed by external staff; and
- sharing traditional manual binding, carried on off-site with automated binding carried on on-site.

After much thinking, the fourth solution was adopted.

The first reason was merely financial: the fourth scenario was the least expensive. The second reason was the economic situation of the binding sector, already mentioned. The third reason was that, from 1991 to 1993, the BnF had conducted several technical studies to improve automated bookbinding, taking into consideration both the preservation requirements and access. That means good ability for books to be opened for photocopying purposes, and a stronger, easier to clean cover.

As it seemed impossible that the result of these studies could be accepted and used by the binders, the library had no choice, but to do it itself. On the other hand, traditional manual binding was the strong point of the French binders with a good cost/quality ratio.

Therefore, in 1994, it was decided to implement an on-site workshop dedicated to automated binding for some 120,000 books per year and to allot some 55,000 books for manual binding to the private sector. The total of the 175,000 books took into account both the needs of all new books and of those which had been waiting to be bound for a long time.

The estimated medium price was FRF 125 (about 19 euros) for internal automated binding and FRF 220 (33 euros) for external manual binding, excluding leather binding. If we look at the investment budget of the library, FRF 10 million (1,5 million euros) were devoted to the equipment of the workshop, and at the same time 35 people were appointed. That was in 1994.

Since that year, two factors have changed the situation. The first one was total hostility from the binders' professional association which was afraid that the project would deprive them of a part of the market. However, they were not ready to update themselves, and only felt concerned about the protection of their century-old craft. So for many years, a long struggle has been waged with the corporation determined to use all the means at its disposal to stop the project through lobbying, including use of the media to convince the general public of the will of the library to put them to death.

The corporation also forged many contacts with the Ministry of Culture and the Ministry of Industry, explaining to the first that it did not fall within a library scope to bind, and compelling the second to defend small firms.

Finally, in 1997, an agreement was officially reached between the Ministry of Culture, responsible for the BnF, and the Ministry of Industry, defender of the private sector. This agreement allowed the library to implement the planned workshop, but limited the production capacity down to 50,000 books per year: that was almost half of what was planned, but it allowed the library to produce a significant quantity of binding, with very innovating technical requirements and shorter lead times.

Fortunately, along with that agreement, there was no parallel fall of the investment budget, necessary for the technical and profitability improvements. The reduction was effective only on the forecast of staffing levels which decreased from 35 to 18 people.

The second factor which modified the 1994 situation was the natural development of the market due to important call for tenders the library had to use to prepare the opening of the reading rooms before the opening of its own binding workshop. At the very beginning, in 1991, that represented some 600,000 books to be purchased, catalogued and bound before the opening of the new building, initially planned for 1995. These books were planned for free-access reading and had to complement the traditional collection of 10-11 million books stored in the stacks.

Between 1991 and 1998, a mere 500,000 books were purchased, but that was essential to prepare a very important call for tenders for the binding of such an amount of books. One of the consequences of the French binders' situation, described above, was that for the last six years - from 1993 to 1998 - half of the books which were to be bound have been sent to a Scottish binder.

Only two French binders have invested enough money to be ready to answer our tenders and only these binders could now offer realistic prices. These binders had to disagree partly with their corporation, which preferred to look down on our tender - which was the tender of the century for them - rather than making technical or economic efforts to be able to meet the demand. Today, the prices of these two binders, in our tender dated 1998, are now significantly lower than the Scottish ones. As a consequence, books are not sent to Scotland any longer. This fall in price can be explained by the end of the investment amortization and by the recognition that fair competition is better than systematic self-centred opposition.

That also has consequences on the organization and the working of our on-site workshop: as the medium price is now around FRF 100 (15 euros), it is unrealistic to hope to be economically better than the private sector, and that will be even more difficult if our production capacity is to decrease.

Therefore, it was decided to reinforce our objective of quality, particularly in terms of production lead times: with off-site binders, it seems impossible to go below three months, including internal preparation. In contrast, it is hoped to bind on-site within one or two weeks.

We are improving new techniques or processes to conserve materials, such as treatments for free access maps, documents coming with CDs, mobile bindings documents which cannot be bound in the traditional way (newspapers, plate collections, brochures, leaflets...). In the long term we also aim in to get production management quality label

So, where are we today? More than half of our equipment is now working with 10 staff. Since 1997, the first automated bindings of on-site production have been completed. We are very proud of this, especially after all those years of battle.

Marie-Lise Tsagouria
Conservation Department
Bibliothèque nationale de France
Paris, France

[Ms Tsagouria's paper was presented at the Seminar, "Preservation Management: Between Policy and Access", held in The Hague, Netherlands, 19-21 April 1999.]

Marie-Thérèse Varlamoff and George MacKenzie

Archives and Libraries in Times of War: The Role of IFLA and ICA within ICBS (International Committee of the Blue Shield)

"Lost Memory"

In 1996, in the framework of its "Memory of the World", programme UNESCO implemented a survey on libraries and archives destroyed in the 20th century. This survey was conducted in cooperation with IFLA and ICA and published under the title of *Lost Memory* by Hans van der Hoeven and Joan van Albada. The list of the libraries that have been totally or partially destroyed is appalling: to quote just a few

- 1923: an earthquake destroyed the Imperial University Library in Tokyo causing the loss of some 700,000 volumes.
- 1933-1935: the Nazis were ordered to prepare black lists of prohibited authors, which represented 10% of public libraries collections. Many of these books were burnt.
- Between 1939 and 1945: In Czechoslovakia, entire collections were confiscated, dispersed and destroyed, including card catalogues. Total losses were estimated at two million volumes. In Poland, the National Library in Warsaw was completely destroyed and 700,000 volumes lost. One-third of all German books were destroyed, although the most precious works have been preserved by storage off-site. One hundred million books have been destroyed in the Soviet Union.
- 1966: In Florence, nearly two million volumes were flooded, although an international rescue operation managed to salvage many of them.
- 1966-1976: In China, during the Cultural Revolution, all libraries were closed for various lengths of time. Some were burnt, others purged, only the books by Marx, Lenin and Mao were spared.

More recently we must recall the fire, deliberately set, which in 1986 destroyed the Los Angeles Central Library and caused the loss of 400,000 volumes, and the fire that devastated the Art Library of the Academy of Sciences in Leningrad in 1988 and damaged 3.6 million books and 400,000 newspapers. We all remember the dramatic vision of the flames raging out of the windows of the National Library of Sarajevo, destroying 90% of the written heritage of the Bosnian Culture.

The UNESCO survey analyzes the various causes of destruction and damage. Apart from war, the ranking of significant dangers are: fire, accidental of criminal; water from outside or inside; earthquakes; civil disorders; and also insects and rodents, mold and humidity, poor storage, neglect, poor restoration, destruction by administrative order. An analysis of implemented and intended measures in the five continents to protect libraries from disasters complete this study.

The 1954 Hague Convention

Conscious of the extent and importance of the destruction that had affected the world's cultural heritage during World War II, UNESCO prepared a Convention for the Protection of Cultural Property in the Event of Armed Conflict, which was adopted in 1954 in The Hague. The 90 State Parties who have signed the Convention agreed:

- to adopt preventive measures to protect the cultural heritage not only during war time (it is too late then) but also during peace time;
- to protect and respect cultural heritage in case of armed conflicts (even when these are not international);
- to create mechanisms to ensure this protection (an international register of cultural items under special protection was created);
- to indicate with a special sign some important buildings; and
- to create special units inside the armed forces in charge of the protection of cultural heritage.

ICBS – International Committee of the Blue Shield

New kinds of conflicts which have broken out in the recent years (Czechoslovakia, Rwanda, Afghanistan, East Timor) and serious natural disasters (like the floods in Florence, 1996, Poland, 1997, or the fires in St Petersburg or Los Angeles, to quote just a few) have led four non-governmental organizations to found the International Committee of the Blue Shield (ICBS). The Blue Shield is the cultural equivalent of the Red Cross. It is the symbol specified in the 1954 Hague Convention for making cultural sites to give them protection from attack in the event of armed conflict.

The International Committee of the Blue Shield (ICBS) covers museums and archives, historic sites and libraries. It brings together the knowledge, experience and international networks of four expert organizations: the International Council of Archives (ICA), the International Council of Museums (ICOM), the International Council on Monuments and Sites (ICOMOS) and the International Federation of Library Associations and Institutions (IFLA). These represent an unrivalled body of expertise to advise and assist in responding to events such as war in former Yugoslavia and hurricane damage in Central America. ICBS is international, independent and professional.

The ICBS works for the protection of the world's cultural heritage, in particular by:
- encouraging safeguarding and respect for cultural property and promoting risk preparedness;
- training experts at national and regional level to prevent, control and recover from disasters;
- facilitating international responses to threats or emergencies threatening cultural property; and
- cooperating with other bodies including UNESCO, ICCROM and the International Committee of the Red Cross (ICRC).

So far, the ICBS has concentrated on two main areas of activity: on training and on the revisions of international law for protecting cultural heritage.

Radenci Declaration

A seminar was held in Radenci, Slovenia, in November 1998 to train personnel to intervene following armed conflict or natural disasters. Participants from 12 countries, drawn from museums, archives, libraries and historic buildings, spent a week discussing strategies and tactics for dealing with disasters. Case studies were presented on war damage in former Yugoslavia, flood damage in Poland, earthquake damage in Italy, together with the experiences of military personnel for the seminar, which was targeted at personnel in eastern and southern Europe.

The seminar drafted a joint statement, to be known in Radenci Declaration calling for:
- the protection, safeguard and respect of cultural property (in both normal and exceptional situations) to be included in national policies and programmes;
- strategies to assess and reduce risk and to improve response capacity in the event of threat to cultural property to be developed; and
- institutions caring for the cultural heritage, to integrate risk preparedness and management within their activities.

New Hague Protocol

The second area of activity of the ICBS has been in the forum of the revision of the Hague Convention. The Convention of 1954 is the main international instrument for protecting cultural heritage in armed conflict, and is based on the idea that the preservation of the cultural heritage is not only a matter for the state in which it is located but is of great importance for all peoples of the world. Since 1954 it has been gradually codified by UNESCO, the UN agency charged with responsibility for cultural matters, and it has also become linked to the development of humanitarian law initiated by the Red Cross.

The Convention reflects the experience of the World War II, a total war between nation states. The majority of conflicts since 1945, which have ravaged cultural property have, however, been of a different type and have often taken place at a sub-national level.

Recognizing the damage to cultural heritage which has taken place despite the existence of the 1954 Convention, a revision process has been underway since 1933, coordinated by UNESCO and with the active participation of the ICRC (International Committee of the Red Cross). The culmination of this process was the March 1999 Diplomatic Conference in The Hague, which agreed a new Protocol giving increased protection and sanctions.

The 1999 Protocol defines clearly the occasions in which "imperative military necessity" can be claimed as a reason for attacking cultural sites. It redefines the obligations on occupying powers regarding cultural property. It creates a new category of exceptional protection to be given to the most important sites and institutions. It introduces a range of new and specific war crimes for breaches, and includes provision for universal international jurisdiction, meaning that such crimes can be prosecuted in any country that signs the Protocol. For the first time, the most serious crimes will be extraditable.

The new Protocol also establishes an inter-governmental committee of states to monitor and review the operation of the Convention. The ICBS, together with the ICRC and ICCROM, is given a specific advisory role to this new committee. The recognition of ICBS in the new protocol is unprecedented, and adds weight to its work in national and international circles.

National Blue Shield Committees

It is vital that the international initiative is taken up and supported by local initiatives. Blue Shield Committees are being formed in a number of countries.

Belgium was the first to do so, and discussions are currently underway in a number of other countries including France, Poland, UK, the Netherlands and Costa Rica. We must note that similar initiatives already exist in Italy, Switzerland, in the USA and the Caribbean.

National Committees can multiply effectiveness by bringing together the different professions, local and national government, the emergency services and the armed forces. They can provide a forum to improve emergency preparedness by sharing experiences and exchanging information. They can provide a focus for raising national awareness of the threats to cultural heritage. They can also promote the ratification and implementation by national governments of the Hague Convention and associated protocols.

The great strength of Blue Shield is that it is cross-sectoral, bringing together professions and institutions across the cultural spectrum. By pooling their expertise, and drawing in military authorities and emergency services, the Blue Shield is a potentially powerful model for managing disaster risks at a national level.

Archives and Libraries Emergency Programmes

Blue Shield is not just an initiative for politically troubled regions of the world. It is highly relevant to the situation we face in relatively stable democratic states. Because armed conflict is deliberate, it may be more damaging to cultural property than natural or accidental damage, but the difference is one of degree and not of principle. The widespread flooding in Poland in 1997 that affected one-third of the country resulted in severe damage to archive and library material and almost overwhelmed the ability of archives and libraries to react. Moreover, steps to mitigate the effects of armed conflict and to protect archives materials, are virtually the same as those to mitigate the effects of other disasters from fire or flood. Studying the problems faced by archives that have experienced armed conflict can help to re-evaluate and improve disaster planning.

In 1997, ICA worked with UNESCO to develop an emergency programme for protecting archives in the event of armed conflict. The programme was based on case studies in three countries in different continents with quite different experiences: Costa Rica, where the constitution forbids an army, the Gambia, where there has been some sporadic armed conflict in the past and Croatia, which experienced severe fighting in 1992.

The emergency programme came to a series of conclusions. The first was that archive institutions must define those of their records (typically 2% to 7%) which are vital and which will receive special attention in protection and salvage. These should normally include all the finding aids. The vital records should also be the subject of special copying programmes and the copies stored remotely.

The second conclusion was that an assessment of risks, based on potential threats, should be at the heart of institutions' policies and programmes. The risk assessment must consider all threats, and balance the seriousness of their impact against the probability of their occurring.

The third conclusion was that protection in situ should always be considered first, and only when it is not possible or appropriate should evacuation of archive material be considered.

The fourth conclusion was that all institutions should establish written emergency policies, fully supported by senior management, with the provision of appropriate materials and equipment. One aspect of the policy must be how to react and survive in conditions where there is little or no infrastructure: in other words, how to be self-sufficient for at least a time.

The final conclusion of the programme was to emphasize the central importance of the archives building. It is the first (or last) line of defense for the archive material and is crucial to the success of any protection programme. The characteristics of the building, its location and construction type need to be examined, its weaknesses need to be analyzed and measures to reduce or overcome them must be devised. Equally, the strengths of the building need to be identified, and exploited.

Although no similar emergency programme has yet been developed between UNESCO and IFLA, the same conclusions can be applied to libraries. IFLA has therefore published a leaflet covering four stages: prevention, preparedness, response and recovery.

Libraries and Archives in Kosovo

Through its constituent organizations, the ICBS has already been active in Kosovo:
- A mission to the national museum of Kosovo in Pristina, jointly mounted by ICOM and "Patrimoine sans frontières" in November 1999.

- A mission to the archives of Kosovo, mounted by ICA in association with UNESCO and the Council of Europe in December 1999.
- A conference of the national directors of archives of former Yugoslavia and neighboring countries, organized by the European Board of ICA in November 1999, which produced a joint declaration.
- Financial assistance was pledged by IFLA to salvage rare manuscripts in December 1999.
- From 25 February to 5 March, 2000 an expert mission mounted by IFLA, UNESCO and the Council of Europe was sent to the main cities of Kosovo in order to prepare an assessment of the situation concerning libraries and to establish rehabilitation guidelines.

A full report on the mission including suggestions for rehabilitation guidelines in short and medium term will soon be available. However a brief report already stated that: "The National and University Library and other special libraries are in decay, the preservation of cultural heritage in terms of printed materials endangered and the national systems to record and disseminate documents are practically out of function. Large parts of the valuable collections in the National and University Library have been removed and probably destroyed during the period 1990-1999."

Many public and school libraries especially in the countryside have been totally burned down, others have had their book collections removed or destroyed, and those which are still functioning suffer from the effects of almost 10 years of neglect in acquisitions. Equally many library books have been burned along with the homes of users. An estimated total of almost half the stocks of all the public libraries are lost. A great part of the remaining books are either outdated or irrelevant to local inhabitants due to their ideological, linguistic or ethnic character. Practically all equipment has been removed and most of the present staff needs training after a long period without professional practice and systematic education.

There is no cooperation or even contact between professionals of the ethnic Albanian majority and professionals in ethnic Serbian enclaves.

In general there is a heavy need for reading rooms, children's literature, current professional literature and access to new technology. International support in terms of funding and professional assistance is now needed to reconstruct libraries and a functioning library network.

Furthermore, an action plan for Kosovo has been drawn. It consists of five main elements:

Assistance with recovery work, both short and long-term:

- compile inventories of cultural property at institutional, regional and national level;
- assess the condition of the different services, their staff, buildings and equipment;
- provide reports on priority needs of each sector;
- identify short term projects for emergency protection of property at risk and for confidence building; and
- develop long term recovery strategies for each sector and for the territory as a whole;

Empowerment of Kosovan institutions and their staffs to improve emergency preparedness and recovery capacity:

- set up mechanism for dialogue between cultural heritage institutions and the military and civil administrations in Kosovo;
- provide cross-sectoral training in risk preparedness and recovery, possibly following the model used in Radenci, Slovenia, in November 1998; and
- encourage the setting up of a Blue Shield Committee in Kosovo, bringing together staffs from the different sectors to promote exchange of experiences and pooling of resources.

Development of staff of cultural heritage institutions and their re-integration into the international community:

- establish dialogue between professional staffs in Kosovo and in neighboring countries;
- encourage attendance of Kosovan staff at international conferences; and
- identify training opportunities for staff, both in Kosovo and abroad.

Promotion of the implementation of the Hague Convention and the new Protocol by all parties involved in the region:

- establish dialogue between proposed national Blue Shield Committee and KFOR; and
- provide specialized training for military and police commanders in Kosovo on the international rules governing protection of cultural property and on their importance of such property.

Raising awareness of the international community of the importance of cultural property and the need to protect it:

- identify potential donors among aid agencies, governments and private foundations;
- establish collaborative partnerships with other concerned organizations, including Patrimoine sans Frontières and the Packard Foundation;
- provide information on protection of Kosovan cultural property through the ICBS Web site; and
- publicize project successes.

It is clear that this action plan will be implemented only if adequate funding is found.

To Mark or Not to Mark?

Last but not least, one question arises frequently in discussion: does using the Blue Shield symbol help to protect the building or site, or does it, as some recent experience indicates, mark it out as a target for hostile forces? The following comment was made by Croatian archivists in 1997: "During the war in Croatia it was obvious that cultural objects were deliberate targets in spite of distinct signs of the Hague Convention. This is an open international problem that calls for changes to the Hague Convention".

Whilst recognizing the danger, the ICBS is strongly in favor of marking, since without it the full protection of international law will not be available to cultural sites and their contents. After all, the Red Cross symbol has on occasions been attacked in 20th Century conflicts, yet there is no suggestion that it should not be used.

Marie-Thérèse Varlamoff
IFLA-PAC Director
Paris, France

George MacKenzie
ICA Deputy Secretary General
Paris, France